THEMATIC UNIT
REVOLUTIONARY WAR

Written by John and Patty Carratello

Illustrated by Cheryl Buhler and Sue Fullam

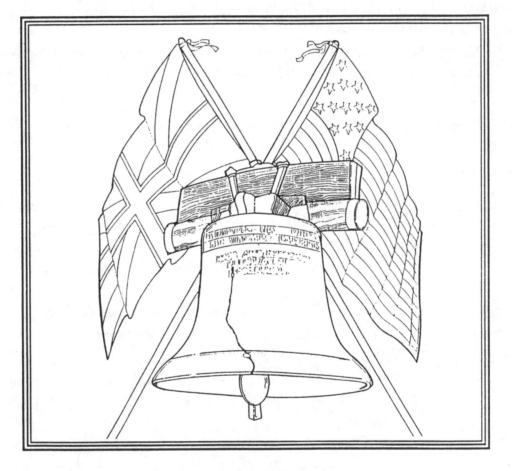

Teacher Created Materials, Inc.
P.O. Box 1040
Huntington Beach, CA 92647
©1991 Teacher Created Materials, Inc.
Made in U.S.A.

ISBN 1-55734-293-8

Table of Contents

Introduction

The Revolutionary War contains a stimulating whole language, thematic unit about a fascinating period in United States history. Its 80 reproducible pages are filled with a wide variety of lesson ideas designed for use with intermediate and junior high school children. At its core are two high-quality children's literature selections, *Johnny Tremain* and *The Fighting Ground*. For each of these books, activities are included which set the stage for reading, encourage the enjoyment of the book, and extend the concepts learned. In addition, the theme is connected to the curriculum with activities in language arts (including daily writing activities), math, science, social studies, art, music, and life skills. Many of these activities encourage cooperative learning. Unit management tools, such as suggestions and patterns for bulletin boards and a research center allow students to synthesize their knowledge and produce products that can be shared in and outside the classroom.

This thematic unit includes:

☐ **literature selections**—summaries of two children's books with related lessons and reproducible pages that cross the curriculum

☐ **poetry and drama**—suggested selections and lessons that enable students to write, perform, and publish their own works

☐ **planning guides**—suggestions for sequencing lessons for the unit

☐ **writing ideas**—daily suggestions, as well as writing activities across the curriculum, including Big Books

☐ **bulletin board ideas**—suggestions and plans for student-created and interactive bulletin boards

☐ **homework suggestions**—extending the unit to the child's home

☐ **curriculum connections**—in language arts, math, science, social studies, art, music, and life skills

☐ **group projects**—to foster cooperative learning

☐ **culminating activities**—which require students to synthesize their learning, to engage in activities and produce products that can be shared with others

☐ **a bibliography**—suggesting additional literature and nonfiction books relating to the theme

---

To keep this valuable resource intact so that it can be used year after year, you may wish to punch holes in the pages and store them in a three-ring binder.

Introduction *(cont.)*

Why Whole Language?

A whole language approach involves children in using all modes of communication: reading, writing, listening, observing, illustrating, experiencing, and doing. Communication skills are interconnected and integrated into lessons that emphasize the whole of language rather than isolating its parts. The lessons revolve around selected literature. Reading is not taught as a separate subject from writing and spelling, for example. A child reads, writes, speaks, listens, and thinks in response to a literature experience introduced by the teacher. In this way, language skills grow naturally, stimulated by involvement and interest in the topic at hand.

Why Thematic Planning?

One very useful tool for implementing an integrated whole language program is thematic planning. By choosing a theme with correlating literature selections for a unit of study, a teacher can plan activities throughout the day that lead to a cohesive, in-depth study of the topic. Students will be practicing and applying their skills in meaningful contexts. Consequently, they will tend to learn and retain more. Both teachers and students will be freed from a day that is broken into unrelated segments of isolated drill and practice.

Why Cooperative Learning?

Besides academic skills and content, students need to learn social skills. No longer can this area of development be taken for granted. Students must learn to work cooperatively in groups in order to function well in modern society. Group activities should be a regular part of school life and teachers should consciously include social objectives as well as academic objectives in their planning. The teacher should clarify and monitor the qualities of good group interaction just as he/she would clarify and monitor the academic goals of the project.

Why Big Books?

An excellent cooperative, whole language activity is the production of Big Books. Groups of students, or the whole class, can apply their language skills, content knowledge, and creativity to produce a Big Book that can become part of the classroom library to be read and reread. These books make excellent culminating projects for sharing beyond the classroom with parents, librarians, and others. Big Books can be produced in many ways, and this thematic unit book includes directions for several methods you may choose.

Johnny Tremain

by Esther Forbes

Summary

In the time of colonial America, Johnny Tremain works as an apprentice to a silversmith, learning the trade with excellence. This young boy is so skilled, he proves himself invaluable to the family to which he is apprenticed, using his artistic skill, management sense, and responsible ways to keep the business thriving.

But when a jealous co-worker hands Johnny a cracked crucible, Johnny's right hand is severely burned by the molten silver which escapes, crippling him and bringing to a halt his promising career.

Burdened with his handicap, he half-heartedly seeks other employment. When unsuccessful, he sinks gloomily into despair. It is Rab, a printer at The Boston Observer, who lifts Johnny up, showing him that he is whole and can be useful serving his country in tremendous ways. Rab and Johnny enter the world of the American Revolutionary War—a world inhabited by Paul Revere, John Hancock, Samuel Adams, and Doctor Warren. This is the world of the Boston Tea Party, Lexington, and Concord. Through the eyes of Johnny Tremain, we see what it might have been like in Boston in the 1770's as witnesses to the birth of a new nation, a new idea.

Each of the lessons suggested below can take from one to several days to complete.

Sample Plan

Lesson 1

- Introduce students to the Revolutionary War period (page 6).
- Assemble Revolutionary War diaries (pages 29 and 30).
- Read Section I of *Johnny Tremain*
- Discuss the role of Apprenticeship (page 8).
- Ask students to complete their own Family Trees (page 55).
- Begin Revolutionary War Research Center Activities (page 72).
- Introduce Big Book options (page 41).

Lesson 2

- Begin Daily Writing Activities (pages 29 to 33).
- Work on Research Center Activities.
- Discuss and share Family Heirlooms (page 56).
- Design Family Crests (pages 56 and 57).
- Read Sections II and III.
- Discuss proportion and scale (page 42).
- Make Clay Sculptures (page 56).

Lesson 3

- Continue Daily Writing Activities
- Work on Research Center Activities.
- Simulate crippled hand (pages 10 and 11).
- Read Sections IV and V.
- Discuss Johnny's care of Goblin (page 50).
- Point out the importance of thinking before you speak and act (pages 9 and 63).
- Set up Committees of Correspondence (page 13).

Lesson 4

- Continue Daily Writing Activites
- Work on Research Center Activities.
- Discuss positive self-image (page 12).
- Read sections VI and VII.
- Work with students to determine what are some important things in their lives, and what they would be willing to do to have these things (page 14).
- Compare the account of the Boston Tea Party and its aftermath as told in *Johnny Tremain* with the account presented in history books.

Sample Plan *(cont.)*

Lesson 5

- Continue Daily Writing Activities.
- Work on Research Center Activities.
- Read Section VIII.
- Investigate the Patriots' treatment of the Tories as reported in history books. Discuss if the type of treatment the Lyte family received corresponds with these historical accounts.
- Discuss the sacrifices people make for what they believe.
- Respond to James Otis' explanation for the Revolutionary War (page 15).

Lesson 6

- Continue Daily Writing Activities.
- Work on Research Center Activities.
- Introduce the game (pages 43 and 44).
- Read sections IX and X.
- Characterize the "enemy" in light of how Johnny felt about the British soldiers he knew.
- Discuss the importance and effectiveness of weapons during the Revolutionary War.
- Chart a contemporary route for Paul Revere's ride (page 46).

Lesson 7

- Continue Daily Writing Activities.
- Work on Research Center Activities.
- Read Section XI and XII.
- Do Picture This! (page 56).
- Learn, sing, and write variations for "Yankee Doodle" (page 60).
- Compare the events of April 18 and 19, 1775 as presented in *Johnny Tremain* and in historical references.
- Do and make a Revolutionary War Crossword Puzzle (pages 37 and 38).

Lesson 8

- Continue Daily Writing Activities.
- Complete Research Center and Bulletin Board Activities (pages 70 to 77).
- Reflect on the differences between Johnny's life as a Patriot and as an apprentice (page 61).
- Project what might happen to characters from *Johnny Tremain* after the war is over (page 16).
- Complete the *Johnny Tremain* Big Books (page 41).
- Read more stories set in the Revolutionary War time period (pages 7, 35, and 78).

Overview of Activities

SETTING THE STAGE

1. **Assemble the bulletin board** (see pages 74 to 77) for students to complete as the unit progresses.

2. **Construct the research center** (see pages 72 and 73), which includes a display of literature and other materials about the Revolutionary War that will appeal to all reading levels. (See Bibliography on page 78 for suggested titles). Encourage students to read these materials during silent reading time or when they have free time between daily assignments and activities.

3. **Help students assemble diaries** (see pages 29 and 30) so they will be ready to make their entries.

4. **Familiarize students with the sights and sounds of the Revolutionary War period** by showing pictures, playing music, and singing songs appropriate to the time, as well as reading historical accounts of the war. (See Bibliography, page 78.)

5. **Introduce *Johnny Tremain*.** Have students define *apprentice*. Discuss what it means to have pride in what one does. Ask students if they think they could function without the use of their writing hand. Ask them if they would risk their lives for their beliefs. Tell them that the main character in the story does all these things, as well as learns that he can make a difference in a new country's struggle for freedom.

Overview of Activities *(cont.)*

1. **Begin to read** *Johnny Tremain.* Discuss what Boston must have been like in the early 1770s, with its programs of apprenticeship, its poverty, and wealth, the characters from history that lived in the city, the Loyalists and the Patriots, and the political controversy that existed there. Do Apprenticeship (page 8), complete family trees (page 55), discuss heirlooms (page 56), and design family crests (pages 56 and 57). Make clay sculptures, and relate proportion and scale to the making of these models (pages 42 and 56).

2. **Introduce Attendance Graphing** (pages 32 and 33), which may be used throughout the unit in conjunction with Revolutionary War Diary activities (pages 29 and 30).

3. **Introduce and explain the research center.** Then begin the activities, which include the Culminating Activities (pages 64 to 69). Student enjoyment of the story will be heightened through research activities that will increase their knowledge and understanding of the time period in which the story takes place. The activities may be done individually or in groups. They may also be done as a class assignment or as homework.

4. **After reading each chapter, have students predict what will happen next.** Students must use their knowledge of the characters and understand the situations they face in order to make realistic predictions. It will also stimulate their interest in reading to find out what happens.

5. **Begin constructing Big Books** (page 41), if students are doing a chapter-by-chapter or section-by-section interpretation. Otherwise, wait until the story is finished.

6. **Begin What If?** (page 31), which gives students an opportunity to create make-believe dialogues between the people they ''meet'' during their reading of Revolutionary War history and literature.

1. **Make** *Johnny Tremain* **Big Books** (page 41) if you have not done so already.

2. **Have students research Revolutionary War** history and share what they have learned with the class.

3. **Distribute the Across the Curriculum activities** that have not been assigned during the reading of *Johnny Tremain,* such as Fast Facts (page 34), Do It! (page 36), Ben Franklin-Scientist (page 48), Revolutionary War Fact Finders (page 51), and Where Did It Happen? (page 45).

4. **Read** *Sarah Bishop,* **another historical fiction selection set in the time of the Revolutionary War.** This story, by Scott O'Dell, is based upon the life of Sarah Bishop, a young girl who becomes a fugitive from the British army and is forced to survive on her own in the wilderness. (See Bibliography, page 78). Compare this strong-willed female protagonist with Johnny Tremain, and relate their experiences to Revolutionary War history.

5. **Read the poems ''Paul Revere's Ride'' by Henry Wadsworth Longfellow and ''Concord Hymn'' by Ralph Waldo Emerson.** Read also the famous writing of patriots, such as Thomas Jefferson's *The Declaration of Independence.* (See Bibliography on page 78.)

6. **Complete the culminating activities** (pages 64 to 69) and invite parents, other classes, and community members to experience what your students have learned and created.

Apprenticeship

In the times when colleges and trade schools were not available, a common way of learning a trade (skilled work) was to become apprenticed to a person skilled in that trade, called the *master craftsman.*

Typically, there would be a legal agreement between the apprentice and the master craftsman. The apprentice worked for the master craftsman for a specified number of years and in return, was trained by the master. During that time the young apprentice would become a part of the master's family.

Today, the word apprentice simply refers to anyone who is a beginner or a learner.

Directions

1. Have your teacher invite members of your community to speak to your class about the kind of work they do. Give your teacher some ideas of the kind of work in which you are interested.

2. Prepare a list of questions to ask the speaker before he or she arrives.

    Here are some sample questions:

    How long have you done this kind of work?

    When did you first decide you wanted to do this?

    What kind of jobs did you do before?

    How long does it take to be able to do what you do?

    What kind of training did you have?

    What is your typical day like?

    Do people apprentice in your kind of work?

3. Take a class survey to find out who in your class would like to do the same kind of work.

8

Think Before You Speak!

Because of Rab, Johnny Tremain became aware of how his actions affected those around him. One time as the two boys sat in Rab's attic toasting cheese and muffins, the older boy said to Johnny, ''Why do you go out of your way to make bad feeling?''

Johnny had no answer for Rab, and no answer for himself. He was quick to ''blow a fuse,'' to act and speak without thinking about the consequences of his actions or words. Rab's question forced Johnny to think about his way of interacting with people. He began to watch his behavior, and learned to better control himself.

1. What was one technique Johnny used to make sure he gave himself time to think before he said or did anything he might later regret?

    _____

    _____

2. What was one of the rewards he reaped because he gave himself time to ''cool off '' before reacting?

    _____

    _____

3. What do you usually say or do when you are angry with another person?

    _____

    _____

4. What usually happens when you react this way?

    _____

    _____

On the back of this paper, write about the changes that would likely happen in your life if you always took the time to think before you acted or spoke.

What's It Like?

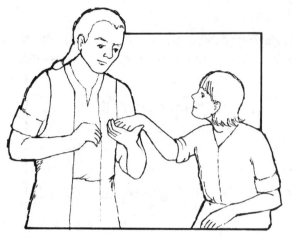

Johnny was forced to make many adjustments, like relearning how to write when he lost the full use of his right hand.

What would it be like without the full use of one of your hands?

Directions

1. Restrict the use of your writing hand by binding your thumb to the palm of your hand with strong tape. Do not remove the tape for the duration of the experiment.

2. Do **not** choose a time of day in which you **must** have the use of both hands to meet any responsibilities like test-taking, team sports, or music lessons.

3. Do **not** choose a time when the use of both hands is unnecessary, such as the time you listen to music, watch TV, or sleep.

4. Perform your daily routines without the full use of your writing hand. Try to adapt the way you do things in order to function successfully.

5. After the experiment is over, complete the record sheet found on page 11.

What's It Like? *(cont.)*

Experiment Recording Form

Name:	
Date and time of experiment:	
Hand I most often use:	

Activities I WAS NOT able to do without the full use of my writing hand:

Activities I WAS able to do without the full use of my writing hand:

Activities I COULD do if I made modifications in the way I did them:

Activities	Modifications I Made

Observations and Conclusions:

A Reflection of You

Johnny was ashamed of his hand. He felt others were disgusted by his injury and shunned him because of it.

What happened to Johnny at the dance in Lexington to help him understand more about his role in how others perceived his hand?

_____

_____

What advice did Rab have for Johnny about his hand?

_____

_____

People can only see you as positively as you see yourself. It is up to you to give people the idea of who you really are. If you see yourself negatively, so will others. If you see yourself positively, so will others.

On the back of this page, list all the things about yourself that you like. Share your list with a family member or close friend. Ask that person if there is anything you can add to your list. Include these suggestions!

Then make a list of things about yourself you do not like. Next to each one, write a suggestion of how you can work to change this thing about yourself you do not like. If it is something that you cannot change, write how you can change your negative attitude about it. Share this list with the same family member or friend. Ask this person for his or her comments about what you have written. Remember, if you like yourself first, others will follow!

12

Committees of Correspondence

Samuel Adams employed Johnny Tremain to ride Goblin and deliver messages around the countryside for the Boston Committee of Correspondence.

In 1772, the first Committee of Correspondence began in Boston, and it was Samuel Adams who started this committee. Soon, other Committees of Correspondence were organized throughout the colonies, before and during the Revolutionary War. The purpose of these committees was to serve as a network of communication between the colonial towns in order to keep abreast of any news that related to British infringement upon the rights of the colonists. These committees played a significant role in pulling the colonists together in their struggle for independence from British rule.

Set up your own "Committees of Correspondence" in your classroom, grade, school, neighborhood, or community. Work in small groups to create correspondence "chains" through which people can keep abreast of important news.

Here are some ideas that can help you get started:

1. Select three to four members for each group.

2. Appoint one or two of the members to collect news, another to write the correspondence, and another to deliver the news to other groups.

3. Decide with whom you want to correspond.

4. Establish ways to deliver your correspondence (by mail, by hand, by bicycle, by skateboard, by carrier pigeon, etc.).

5. Evaluate the successfulness of your news-spreading system.

6. Based on your own experience with "Committees of Correspondence" and the reading you have done about the historical Committees of Correspondence, evaluate the effectiveness of committees such as these for spreading news in the time before and during the Revolutionary War.

Wants vs. Principles

When the Americans dumped the tea from a British ship into Boston Harbor, they proved that they were more concerned about a principle than in saving money on something that was a very important part of their lives. Even though the tea was better and less expensive than any other tea they could buy, they refused to pay the small tax placed on the tea by Britain's Parliament. The colonists did not want to be taxed at all, unless they could have a voice in the ways taxes could be levied upon them. They would not sell out for anything because their beliefs were so strong.

Where would you draw the line between your principles and your wants?

Suppose you, like the colonists, disagreed with a tax that was being imposed upon you. The tax is levied upon things that are very important to you, and you know you will have a hard time living your "normal" life without these things.

Read the items in the box below. Divide them into two columns. In the left column, list those things you could not live without and would pay a tax, even though paying this tax was against your principles. In the right column, list those things you would "throw overboard" rather than pay a tax.

television	chips	Nintendo	basketball
pizza	bicycle	comic books	stuffed animal
baseball cards	doll	radio	jewelry
sunglasses	soap	hair dryer	designer clothes
soda	computer	gum	French fries
calculator	jeans	tea	records or tapes

STOP! I'LL PAY!	GO AHEAD! I'LL NEVER PAY!

That A Man Can Stand Up

At their last meeting in the attic, James Otis tells the Observers the simple reason for the impending war with England.

*"We give all we have, lives, property, safety, skills . . .
we fight, we die, for a simple thing. Only that a man can stand up."*

Directions

1. Read the above quote to the entire class.

2. As a class or in small groups, have your students consider and discuss the following questions. Encourage students to explain their thinking to one another.

  * What does James Otis mean by these words?

  * Do you think that the men who heard Otis say these words believed as James Otis did about this reason for the Revolutionary War? Single out individual Patriots as you respond to this question if you feel that not all of the listeners felt the same way.

  * Do you agree with James Otis as to the reason for the war?

  * Do you think this "simple" reason is one that justifies going to war where many people on both sides will be killed?

  * Would **you** fight a war so "a man can stand up?"

  * For what would you fight and possibly lose your life? List as many reasons as possible.

  * What are the three most important things you would die for? List them in order of importance to you.

Invite some war veterans to class. Encourage them to explain their reasons for going to war. Ask these men and women what they think of fighting so that a man or woman can stand up?

The War Is Over–Now What?

The Revolutionary War finally came to an end with the signing of the Treaty of Paris in 1783.

What do you think the lives of the characters you met in Johnny Tremain might have been like after the war? Work in groups to create dialogues for what you think might have happened if one or more of the combinations of characters listed below had met. Perform your dialogues for the class.

Johnny Tremain and Priscilla Lapham

Mrs. (Lapham) Tweedie and Mr. Percival Tweedie

General Gage and Lieutenant Stranger

Goblin and Johnny

Paul Revere and Johnny Tremain

Merchant Lyte, Lavinia Lyte, and Johnny Tremain

*Paul Revere, James Otis, John Hancock,
Dr. Warren, Sam Adams, John Adams*

Dove and Johnny Tremain

Madge and Sergeant Gale

Lavinia Lyte and Isannah Lapham

Johnny Tremain and Doctor Warren

16

The Fighting Ground

by Avi

Summary

For a thirteen-year-old boy filled with the pride of patriotism and dreams of glory, fighting in the American Revolutionary War is a glamorous and coveted induction into manhood. When the call to arms is sounded, Jonathan joins others from his town and eagerly sets off to battle against the wishes of his parents.

__The Fighting Ground__ is a chronicle of the twenty-four hours that Jonathan experiences as a soldier. It is his story of war and the external and internal battles he faces. By the end of the story Jonathan discovers that the life of a soldier is a life he no longer desires. This book gives a realistic, unglorified, and compassionate view of how war was and can be for all who experience it.

Each of the lessons suggested below could take from one to several days to complete.

Sample Plan

Lesson 1

- Introduce students to the Revolutionary War period (page 18).
- Assemble Revolutionary War diaries (pages 29 and 30).
- Read *The Fighting Ground,* Sections 9:58, 10:15, 10:25, 10:45, 11:00, and 11:30.
- Practice writing in a timed-entry journal style, as used in *The Fighting Ground* (page 20).
- Discuss obedience to parents (page 21).
- Begin Revolutionary War Research Center Activities (page 70).
- Introduce Big Book options (page 41).

Lesson 2

- Begin Daily Writing Activities (pages 29 to 33).
- Work on Research Center Activities.
- Read sections 12:05, 12:30, 12:40, 12:50, 1:00, 1:05, 1:30, 2:05, 2:10, 2:30, and 2:35.
- Determine where the story took place (page 22).
- Discuss the levels of endurance it takes to march a long distance carrying a heavy load (page 49).

Lesson 3

- Continue Daily Writing Activities
- Work on Revolutionary War Research Center Activities.
- Read Sections 2:40, 2:41, 2:50, 3:01, 3:05, 3:16, 3:30. 3:35, 3:38, and 3:47.
- Define *Hessians* (page 23).
- Discuss how Jonathan feels about the "glory of battle" now.
- Create a montage of war (page 56).

Lesson 4

- Continue Daily Writing Activities
- Work on Revolutionary War Research Center Activities.
- Read Sections 3:50, 4:01, 4:10, 4:30, 5:00, 5:15, 5:20, 5:30 and 5:40.
- Invite someone who knows how to speak German to your class to demonstrate the correct pronounciation of the German phrases used in *The Fighting Ground.*
- Practice using and translating German phrases (pages 24 and 25).
- Build a model of a Swedish style log cabin (page 47).

Sample Plan *(cont.)*

Lesson 5

- Continue Daily Writing Activities
- Work on Revolutionary War Research Center Activities.
- Read Sections 6:00, 6:35, 6:45, 7:00, 7:35, 7:40, 8:15, 8:45, 9:00, and 9:15 .
- Ask students to point out instances of compassion shown by the Hessians and by Jonathan.
- Discuss the innocent victims of war.
- Introduce the *Scavenger Hunt* game (pages 51 and 54).

Lesson 6

- Continue Daily Writing Activities
- Work on Revolutionary War Research Center Activities.
- Read Sections 9:30, 9:45, 10:10, 10:15, 11:30, 11:25, 11:35, and 11:50.
- Discuss the external and internal battles that Jonathan fought in *The Fighting Ground* (page 28).

- Make johnnycake (page 62).
- Defend or condemn the actions of the Corporal toward the French Papists.
- Create a Revolutionary War game board (pages 51 to 53).

Lesson 7

- Continue Daily Writing Activities
- Complete the Revolutionary War Research Center Activities (pages 72 and 73) and the Bulletin Board Activities (pages 74 to 77).
- Exchange Revolutionary War game boards and play board games with classmates.
- Read Sections 12:30, 4:30, 5:00, 5:30, 5:35, 5:38, 5:45, 5:50, 6:10, 6:13, 6:40, 9:30, and 10:30.
- Give opinions of Jonathan's and the Corporal's actions.
- Discuss the change in attitude toward war that was revealed through Jonathan's actions, words, and thoughts (pages 26 and 27).
- Read more stories set in the Revolutionary War time period (pages 19, 35, and 78).

Overview of Activities

SETTING THE STAGE

1. **Assemble Independence: A Bulletin Board of People, Places, and Events of the Revolutionary War** for students to complete as the unit progresses. (See pages 74 to 77.)

2. **Construct Independence: A Research Center of People, Places, and Events of the Revolutionary War,** which includes a display of fiction and nonfiction literature, as well as other materials about the Revolutionary War that will appeal to all reading levels. (See Bibliography on page 78 for suggested titles.) Encourage students to read these materials during silent reading time or when they have free time between daily assignments and activities.

3. **Help students assemble their Revolutionary War diaries** so they will be ready to make their entries. (See Revolutionary War Diary, pages 29 and 30.)

4. **Familiarize students with the sights and sounds of the Revolutionary War period** by showing pictures, playing music, and singing songs appropriate to the time, as well as reading historical accounts of the war. (See Bibliography, page 78.)

5. **Introduce *The Fighting Ground*.** Ask students what they think the book will be about, based on hearing the title. Find out the attitudes that students in your classroom have toward war. Ask how many would volunteer to go into battle. Find out if any of your students disobey their parents. What are their attitudes toward, and the consequences of, their disobedience? Tell them about Jonathan, and how he, against the will of his parents, eagerly joined in the fight, and discovered that war was **not** what he thought it would be.

Overview of Activities *(cont.)*

ENJOYING THE BOOK

1. **Begin to read *The Fighting Ground.*** Discuss how Jonathan might have felt as he heard the tavern bell call the men of his town to battle. Describe how he might have felt when he chose to disregard the wishes of his parents. Do the activities: Listen To Your Parents (page 21), 24 Hours (page 20), and Where Am I? (page 22).

2. **Introduce Attendance Graphing** (pages 32 and 33), which may be used throughout the unit in conjunction with Revolutionary War Diary activities (pages 29 and 30).

3. **Introduce and explain the research center.** Then begin the activities which include the Culminating Activities (pages 64 to 69). Student enjoyment of the story will be heightened through research activities that will increase their knowledge and understanding of the time period in which the story takes place. The activities may be done individually or in groups. They may also be done as a class assignment or as homework.

4. **After reading each chapter, have students predict what will happen next.** By predicting what will happen next, students must use their knowledge of the characters and understand the situations they face in order to make realistic predictions. It will also stimulate their interest in reading to find out what happens.

5. **Begin constructing Big Books** (page 41), if students are doing a chapter-by-chapter or section-by-section interpretation. Otherwise wait until the story is finished.

6. **Begin What If?** (page 31), which gives students an opportunity to create make-believe dialogues between the people they "meet" during their reading of Revolutionary War history and literature.

EXTENDING THE BOOK

1. **Make *The Fighting Ground* Big Books** (page 41) if you have not done so already.

2. **Have students research Revolutionary War history,** and share what they have learned with the class.

3. **Distribute the Across the Curriculum activities** that have not been assigned during the reading of *The Fighting Ground*, such as Fast Facts (page 34), Do It! (page 36), and Interact (page 63).

4. **Read *My Brother Sam Is Dead*,** another Revolutionary War period story about a young boy's experience with war and its pain. This Newbery Honor Book is written by James Lincoln Collier and Christopher Collier. (See Bibliography, page 78). Compare the members of the Meeker family and their attitudes toward war with Jonathan's attitudes toward war that are revealed in *The Fighting Ground*. Do Read On! (page 35).

5. **Complete the culminating activities** (pages 64 to 69) and invite parents, other classes, and community members to experience what your students have learned and created.

24 Hours

The Fighting Ground chronicles a full day in the life of a young boy eager to fight in the Revolutionary War. We learn, hour by hour, what Jonathan is doing, feeling and thinking. Because Avi had given us so many details of Jonathan's day, we feel like we are experiencing the war right along with him.

Write an hour-by-hour chronicle of a twenty-four-hour day in your life. Your story could be about a day that holds special meaning for you, like a reunion with favorite friends, a birthday celebration, an unusual family outing, or a significant day for you in sports. Your story could be about a time you were particularly frightened, sad, excited, or embarrassed. You might write about an ordinary day in your life that is filled with everyday things. Whichever type of day you choose to chronicle, be sure to include an hour-by-hour account of what you do, feel, and think.

When you have finished your chronicle, reread it. See if your writing recreates the time vividly for you. If it does not, rework your writing. Include more details. If it does, share your day with a friend or family member. Does this reader feel as if he or she is really there with you? If not, add more description, feeling, or personal observations to your writing. If so, congratulations! You have done a great job!

20

Listen To Your Parents

Upon hearing the tavern bell calling the men in the area to battle, Jonathan yearned to follow its call. His parents, however, had other ideas about Jonathan's involvement in the fight.

What strong words did Jonathan's father say to him that he chose to disobey?

_____

_____

What advice from his mother did Jonathan pretend not to hear?

_____

_____

Why do you think Jonathan chose to disregard his parents' words?

_____

_____

If you had been in Jonathan's place and felt as he did toward fighting in the war, would you have acted in the same way he did? Explain why or why not.

_____

_____

_____

Under what circumstances, if any, might you disobey your parents?

_____

Circle your position on this scale of obedience to parents:

I always obey my parents.	I obey my parents more than disobey them.	I obey my parents about half the time.	I disobey my parents more than I obey them.	I rarely obey my parents.
10 9	8 7	6 5	4 3	2 1

On the back of this page, explain your reasons for the position you circled on the obedience scale above.

Where Am I?

In *The Fighting Ground*, Jonathan mentioned these places he either traveled to or was near. Circle as many of these places as you can on this map of New Jersey. Then, below the map, write any directional or mileage clues for these places that are given in *The Fighting Ground*. Use these clues to mark Jonathan's travel route on the map.

Example: two miles west of tavern

Alexandria: _____   Rocktown: _____

Fleming: _____   Snydertown: _____

Linvale: _____   Trenton: _____

Pennington: _____   Well's Ferry: _____

Put an **X** on the map where you think the tavern might be.

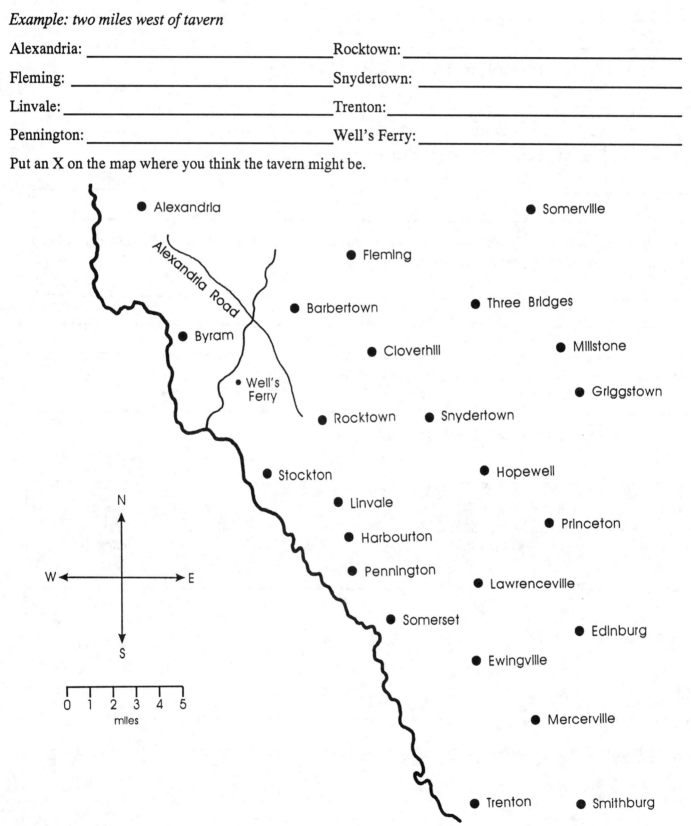

22

The Hessians

The Hessians who battled the American patriots were called mercenaries.

1. What are mercenaries?

   _____

   _____

2. What country was the homeland of the Hessians?

   _____

   _____

3. What kind of reputation did the Hessians have as soldiers?

   _____

   _____

4. How did Jonathan feel toward the three Hessians who captured him?

   _____

   _____

5. How do you think they felt toward Jonathan?

   _____

   _____

6. Why did Jonathan try to save the Hessians?

   _____

   _____

7. Would you have tried to save them if you had been in Jonathan's place? Why?

   _____

   _____

Color this Hessian uniform according to the description given in *The Fighting Ground*.

Steh Auf!

In *The Fighting Ground*, the Hessians speak German. With the help of the translation section in the back of the book, we can understand what is being said.

Here is a dialogue that has been created using the German phrases from the story. Translate it!

David: Steh Auf!

Jason: *(sleepily)* Was war das?

David: Steh Auf!

Jason: *(very sleepily)* Was sagt er?

David: *(loudly)* Los!

Jason: *(confused, and still sleepy)* Woher kommt denn der?

David: Los, beeil dich!

Jason: Noch ein Paar Minuten.

David: *(losing all patience)* Steh auf! Nun komm, beeil dich!

Jason: *(now quite awake, sitting up)* Was gibt's?

David: Das ist besser. Komm hierher, Junge!

Jason: Was gibt's?

David: Los! Mach die Tür auf!

      Both go outside. It is sunrise.

David: Siehst du was?

Jason: Es ist ein schönes Land.

David: Vor unseren Augen.

Unison: Es ist ein schönes Land.

Work with a partner to create another dialogue using the German phrases from the book. Share your dialogue with the class. See if your classmates understand what you say!

Get Up!

In *The Fighting Ground*, the Hessians speak German. With the help of the translation section in the back of the book, we can understand what is being said.

Here is a dialogue that has been created using the English translation of German phrases from the story. Translate it back into German!

David:	Get up!
Jason:	*(sleepily)* What was that?
David:	Get up!
Jason:	*(very sleepily)* What's he saying?
David:	*(loudly)* Come on!
Jason:	*(confused, and still sleepy)* Where did he come from?
David:	Come on, hurry up!
Jason:	A couple more minutes.
David:	*(losing all patience)* Get up! Come on, hurry up!
Jason:	*(now quite awake, sitting up)* What's going on?
David:	That's better. Come here, boy!
Jason:	What's going on?
David:	Go on! Open the door!
	Both go outside. It is sunrise.
David:	Do you see anything?
Jason:	It's a beautiful country.
David:	Right before our eyes.
Unison:	It's a beautiful country.

Work with a partner to create another dialogue using the English phrases for the German used in the book. See if any of your classmates can translate your words into German.

Make It Be a Battle!

With the help of these quotes selected from *The Fighting Ground*, develop an essay which clearly shows the change that Jonathan has undergone in the 24 hours chronicled in the story.

9:58	"Jonathan dreamed of one day taking up a gun himself and fighting the enemy."
10:25	"O Lord, he said to himself, make it be a battle. With armies, big ones, and cannons and flags and drums and dress parades! Oh, he could, *would* fight. Good as his older brother. Maybe good as his pa. Better, maybe. O Lord, he said to himself, make it something *grand!*"
1:30	"They stood watching as the band moved off. Jonathan began to find his pride again. They were, he reminded himself, looking for him, for he too was a soldier. Then, realizing he was being left behind, he bolted down the road."
2:40	"Sweating all over, hoping no one had seen his clumsy slowness, Jonathan glanced about. No one was looking at him."
2:43	"He knew that he had to reload and shoot again, but he stood where he was, confused. Why were things happening so quickly? It was unfair."
3:01	"He ran in terror, straining every muscle, pumping his legs, his arms, not daring to look back."
3:16	"Deep, racking sobs came then, dry and hard. He felt a terrible loneliness. He did not know what he was or what would become of him. He did not know what to do, where to go. All he knew was pain."
4:10	"Jonathan tried to rekindle his hatred, but all he could muster was his desire to stand close to them, to be taken care of. He didn't want to be left out."
4:30	"He began to wonder about what truly had happened when they had fought. He knew they had been beaten. It had been so confused, so wrongly done, it was a wonder that they had even stood and fought at all. It seemed so stupid now"
8:15	"Gradually, it came to him that he could do anything, anything he chose to do. The soldiers, all asleep, were powerless. He could, he knew, simply walk away and be free. He could stay and be their prisoner. Or—he realized with a quickening sense of dread—he could do what any true soldier would do. He could kill them."
8:45	"He tried to pull the trigger. His fingers would not move. He could not shoot."
9:00	"As he lay there, he saw himself as he had been that morning, listening to the tavern bell. The bell! He could feel himself—see himself—so eager to go to battle, to be a hero, to destroy the enemy. It seemed such a long time ago!"
12:30	"Whose side, he asked himself, was he on?"
6:13	"But now his rage had seized him completely, pouring through him. Gripping the gun even tighter, he began pounding it against the stones, again and again and again. The gun stock splintered. The metal bent and burst. Pieces flew in all directions. He fell to his knees sobbing."
10:30	"Oh, how glad he was to be there. And alive. Oh, alive."

26

What Is War?

Throughout *The Fighting Ground*, Avi gives us insight as to the nature of war through the eyes of his characters.

For each character below, write something he or she might say about the war.

Jonathan (April 3, 1778, 9:58 a.m.)

Jonathan's father

Jonathan's mother

A Tory

The Corporal

The tavern keeper

Jonathan's father's friend who was killed

The woman at the water well who gave water to the Corporal and to his troop.

The Frenchman

The old Hessian

The young Hessian

The French Papists (mother and father to the orphan boy)

The orphan boy

Jonathan (April 4, 1778, 10:30 a.m.)

What does war mean to you? How do you feel about it? Compose an essay to express your feelings about war.

Inside and Out

For Jonathan, the war took place on two fighting grounds. One battle was fought physically, between the Hessians and the Corporal's volunteers. The other battle, a psychological one, raged in Jonathan's mind as he struggled to find the **real** enemy.

During the twenty-four hours in which the story takes place, Jonathan discovers that there are real people on both sides in war who have individual personalities, fears, and imperfections. Jonathan was never a victim of the renowned brutality of the Hessians. In fact, he almost befriended them. He was confused by the brutality of the Corporal toward the French Papists because the Corporal was supposed to be a ''good guy.'' Jonathan's sense of loyalty was not clearly defined, and he often wondered whose side he was on.

Suppose Jonathan was given the opportunity to share what he had learned about the war and the enemies he met in war. Which experiences would he share, what would he say about them, and what advice could he give?

Work in groups to prepare his words on war that might be presented to each of the following groups:

* The men at the tavern who gathered there the night of his return from the fighting ground

* A group of Hessians who had been taken prisoners by the Patriots

* The Corporal and a group of his same-minded buddies

* His father and mother

* A group of young children eager to go into battle

* The young French boy whose parents were killed by the Corporal

* The members of your class

Many of us have our own battles raging, both inside and outside of ourselves. As a class, brainstorm a list of things that could cause these internal and external conflicts. Discuss some of these conflicts together.

28

Revolutionary War Diary

Objective

For the duration of your Revolutionary War unit, have each student keep a daily diary. The purpose of the diary is to encourage students to ''bring to life'' this period of American history.

Directions

Each student should have a diary that includes the following:

   * **A Revolutionary War Diary Cover**

Students may create their own, or color and use the one on page 30.

   * **A Daily Entries Section**

Include one page of paper for each day students will be studying the Revolutionary War. You will give them a different topic each day for a daily writing assignment. See Attendance Graphing (pages 32, 33) for a simple way to do this.

You may use the Attendance Graphing questions on page 33 and the Revolutionary War Thought Bank (page 40) for topic ideas, or make up your own. Students may also generate topics for writing.

   * **An Interesting Facts Section**

Include blank pages for students to record any Revolutionary War facts that they find particularly interesting. These facts may come from any reliable source. The facts they collect may also be used for the Fast Facts game (page 34).

   * **A Thoughts and Questions Section**

Include blank pages for students to record their questions and thoughts as they read and learn about the Revolutionary War. Students record their personal feelings about what they learn.

Extension

Encourage your students to bring their diary ideas to life! Ideas generated from their diaries can be used to create plays, debates, stories, songs, and art displays. See What If? (page 31) for one way this can be done.

Diary Cover

What If?

Directions

Tell students that a **dialogue** is a conversation between two or more people.

Have students create a make-believe dialogue between two or more people they have "met" during their reading of Revolutionary War history and literature.

Tell them that it is important that they get "inside" each person as they decide what that person will say. Explain that this will help make the words they give that person sound more believable!

Here are some dialogue ideas you can give them:

* King George III, Samuel Adams, and Benjamin Franklin talk about a peaceful solution to the crisis between England and the colonies.

* A Patriot and a Loyalist actively debate the impending war with England.

* Three members of the Sons of Liberty talk about why and how they will be involved in the Boston Tea Party.

* Paul Revere and William Dawes discuss the night of April 18, 1775.

* Benedict Arnold explains his reasons for becoming a traitor to a distinguished group of Patriots.

* George Washington and Charles Cornwallis meet in a Yorktown restaurant after the war.

* Johnny Tremain travels to London after the war to meet with Jonathan Lyte, Lavinia Lyte, and Isannah.

* Dr. Warren's treatment of Johnny's hand is successful. They discuss Johnny's future.

* Lieutenant Stranger and Johnny Tremain meet at a horse show after the war.

* The boy who rang the bell which called Jonathan to war in *The Fighting Ground*, wants to go to war. He asks Jonathan for his advice.

* Jonathan and the Corporal meet in Rocktown after the war.

* After the war, a family of Hessians settles next to the New Jersey farm of Jonathan and his family. The families meet for the first time.

* List your own dialogue ideas on the back of this page.

Be sure to tell students to practice their dialogues before they present them to the class. Remind them to speak and act as if they really are the people who are talking!

Attendance Graphing

This is a simple way for students to practice writing, listening, and speaking on a daily basis! Students construct a graph, while nametags of absent students remain on the wall, making it easy to take morning attendance. This activity may also be used in conjunction with the **daily entries** section of the students' Revolutionary War diaries. (See pages 29 and 30).

Preparation

Each student will need a name tag that is approximately 2" x 3".

Give each student a piece of double-faced tape, push pin, or magnet to attach his or her name tag to the graph.

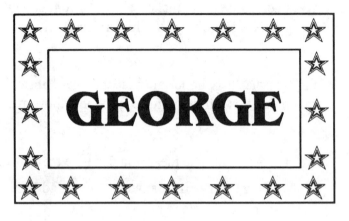

Directions

1. Before students arrive each day, write a Revolutionary War question on the chalkboard or attach one to a bulletin or magnetic board.

2. As they enter the classroom, have students move their name tags from a place on the wall to a place indicating their response to the question of the day. (See example below.)

3. When students get to their seats, have them write down the questions and their response to that question including their **reasons** for that response.

   If you are using this activity to generate the topic for the **daily entries** section of students' Revolutionary War diaries, have students do their writing in their diaries.

4. Later, in cooperative learning groups, students may take turns reading their papers or diary entries to one another in a group "talk-around," following the rules on page 33.

Remaining Students	Would you more likely be a Patriot or a Loyalist?			
Sharon	**Patriot**	Rick	Gina	Veronica	Keith
Susan	**Loyalist**	Donna	Chris	David	
Frank	**Undecided**	Cheryl			

Students will have constructed a graph, while the tags of absent students will remain on the wall, making it easy to take morning attendance.

Attendance Graphing *(cont.)*

Group Talk-Around Rules

* Only one person may speak at a time.

* The person speaking must talk loudly enough for all group members to hear.

* All group members must have eye contact with the speaker and listen courteously.

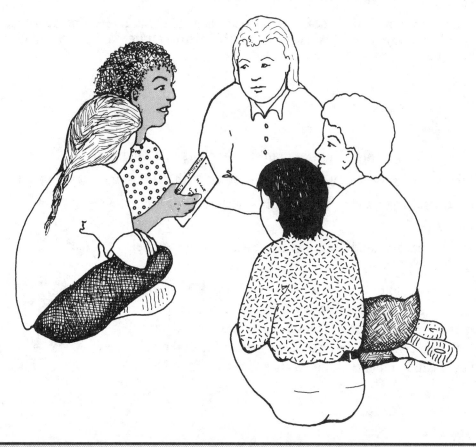

Sample Questions

1. Would you more likely be a Patriot or a Loyalist?

2. Would you use your voice, your pen, or your gun to fight for the things you believe in?

3. Who would you be more apt to be like if you lived during the time of the Revolutionary War: Johnny Tremain or Jonathan from *The Fighting Ground*?

4. Which Revolutionary War leader would you have admired most had you lived during the time of the Revolutionary War: Samuel Adams, Thomas Paine, George Washington, or Benjamin Franklin?

5. Do you think the Revolutionary War could have been avoided?

Fast Facts

If students have been keeping a daily Revolutionary War Diary (page 29), they can use the information from their Interesting Facts section to play a memory game called Fast Facts.

Preparation

- Pass out five blank 3" x 5" cards to each student.
- Have students select and neatly recopy five of their favorite facts from the Interesting Facts section of their diaries on the cards, writing one fact on each card. **Make sure students are writing clear, concise facts, not opinions.**
- Collect all the cards.

Game Directions

1. Divide the class into equal-size teams of no less than six members in each group.

2. Ask each team to arrange themselves in order, with the person with the best memory going last.

3. Each team takes a turn standing or sitting in a straight line across the front of the classroom.

4. The teacher shuffles the fact cards and deals one fact card to each member of the team.

5. The first person in line reads aloud the fact found on the card. The second person repeats the first person's fact and adds the fact from his or her card. The third person repeats the facts in order from the first and second person and adds another fact. This continues until someone makes a mistake or the last team member successfully repeats all the facts and reads his or her own fact card.

IMPORTANT:

Members may not talk once they have had a turn. This is a memory and listening game, so all team members must be listening the first time their teammates recite their facts.

The teams that can recite all their facts win! (You may or may not want to have playoffs to determine a single winning team.)

Play this game over and over again using the same fact cards and adding new ones as your students continue to read and learn more about the Revolutionary War.

Read On!

Students can learn more about the Revolutionary War by reading one or more outstanding books set in this time period. They will become immersed in its history and long remember what they have learned. The Bibliography (page 78) lists some age-appropriate choices.

As a teacher, you may wish to provide an outline for their reading experience. Using the outline, they can then share what they have read with the rest of the class. Here is one outline idea, using the Newbery Honor Book *My Brother Sam Is Dead.*

Outline

Title: *My Brother Sam Is Dead*

Authors: James Lincoln Collier and Christopher Collier

Publisher and

Copyright Date: Macmillan, 1974

About the Book

Give a brief summary of the story.

Sides are not always clearly drawn in wars. Some families are split apart by them. Such is the case of the Meeker family whose divided loyalties during the Revolutionary War form the plot of *My Brother Sam Is Dead.*

Life Meeker, the father of the Meeker family, is a loyal supporter of the King of England. His eldest son, Sam, is fueled by the fire of independence from British rule, and has joined with the Patriots to battle the British forces. The younger son, Tim, who tells the story, is forced to face the political unrest that tears his family and country apart. The story is realistic and moving, filled with choices and their consequences. It is a story of Tim's growth and his difficult road to maturity.

Revolutionary War Connections

Relate the people, places, and events that are mentioned in the story to actual people, places, and events in the Revolutionary War.

Students might research historical characters mentioned in the story, such as Samuel Adams, John Hancock, Benedict Arnold, Isabel Putnam, Tories, Patriots, Minutemen, and Lobsterbacks. They may also choose to report on events found in the story, such as the Battles of Lexington and Concord, and the Long Island raids.

In Your Life

Choose one or more of the events in the story and relate it in some way to your own life.

Students might want to describe how it might be for them if their own families were torn apart by the issues of a war.

Do It!

Divide the class into ten groups. Give one of these cards to each group. Each group follows the instructions on the card it is given. When all the groups are finished, ask them to present their group work to the class.

Groups may try other cards that pique their interest! You may also choose to do any of these cards as an entire class activity.

Describe your life as a Tory in the year 1775. Give as many details as you can.

The Stamp Act of 1765 imposed taxes on American colonists in 55 ways.

Think of 55 ways to be taxed.

John Hancock was famous for his signature.

Practice writing his name in the style of his writing. Have a John Hancock look-alike signature contest.

Design and make an outfit that might have been worn by a person in the Revolutionary War time period.

Have a fashion show.

Describe your life as a Patriot in the year 1775. Give as many details as you can.

Use ice cream sticks or twigs to build your own log cabin.

Draw a flintlock musket. Describe the steps needed to load and fire it.

Think of three non-violent ways you could solve a problem when someone is telling you what to do, and you do not like what that person has told you to do.

Design a map that shows at least ten locations of important places in the Revolutionary War.

Draft a version of your own *Declaration of Independence*, in which you declare yourself free from whatever it is that has been oppressing you.

36

Revolutionary War Crossword Puzzle

In cooperative learning groups of three or four, work together to create **across** and **down** questions that can be used with this crossword puzzle.

For example:

1 across: Who was the British general who surrendered at Yorktown?

3 down: What was the name of the patriotic group of men who helped fuel the Revolution? The _____ of Liberty.

You may want to use the Revolutionary War Word Bank (page 39) to give you more information about first and last names.

Make Your Own Crossword Puzzle

Use this grid to make your own Revolutionary War crossword puzzle. Use words from the Revolutionary War Word Bank (page 39) to help you build your puzzle. Your words may only be written across and down and may not rest on top of, or next to, each other.

Example:

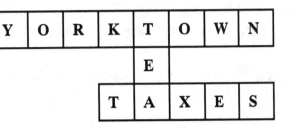

Acceptable   **Not Acceptable**

Write your **across** and **down** clues on a separate piece of paper.

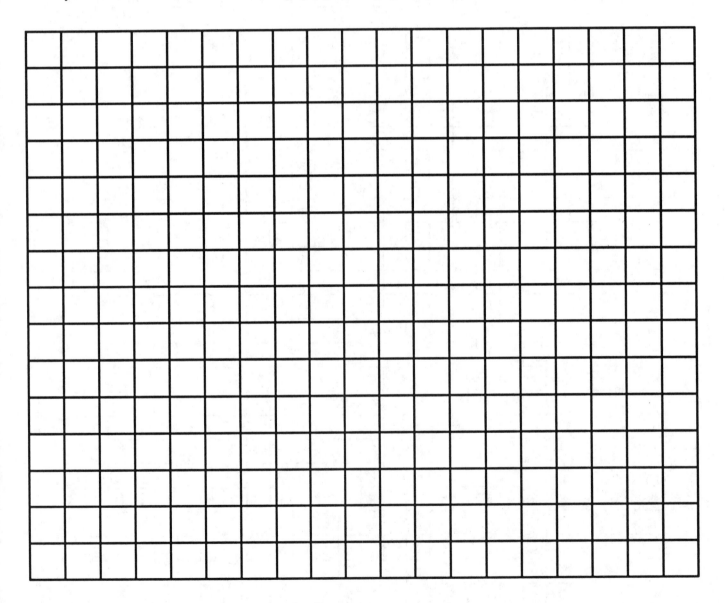

This grid may also be used to create a wordsearch puzzle. Ask your teacher to show you how!

Revolutionary War Word Bank

Use the names and words listed on this page as a resource for Revolutionary War research projects, oral reports, writing assignments, and other activities.

People

Abigail Adams
John Adams (1)
Samuel Adams (1)
Ethan Allen
Benedict Arnold
Crispus Attucks
Boston Observers (1)
John Burgoyne
George Rogers Clark
Henry Clinton
Charles Cornwallis
Lydia Darragh
Daughters of Liberty
William Dawes (1)
John Dickinson
Benjamin Franklin
Thomas Gage (1)
Horatio Gates
Green Mountain Boys
Nathanael Greene
Nathan Hale

John Hancock (1)
Molly (Pitcher) Hays
Patrick Henry
Hessians (2)
Richard Howe
William Howe
Thomas Hutchinson (1)
Thomas Jefferson
John Paul Jones
King George III (1, 2)
Marquis de Lafayette
Richard Henry Lee
Loyalist (1,2)
Francis Marion
Joseph Plumb Martin
mercenary (2)
Daniel Morgan
Lord North
James Otis (1)
Thomas Paine
Patriot (1, 2)

Andrew Pickens
Josiah Quincy (1)
Paul Revere (1)
Jean Baptiste de
   Rochambeau
Betsy Ross
Peter Salem
Deborah Sampson
Sons of Liberty (1)
Thomas Sumter
Tory (1,2)
Charles Townshend
Baron Friedrich
   von Steuben
Joseph Warren (1)
George Washington (2)
Phillis Wheatley
Whig (1)

Places

Beacon Hill
Boston (1)
Brandywine
Bunker Hill
Camden
Charleston
Concord (1)
Cowpens
Delaware River

Fort Ticonderoga
France
Germantown
Germany (2)
Lexington (1)
Long Island (2)
Monmouth
Netherlands
Philadelphia

Poland
Princeton
Rocktown (2)
Saratoga
Savannah
Spain
Trenton (2)
Valley Forge
Yorktown

Things

bayonet (2)
Boston Massacre
Boston Observer (1)
Boston Tea Party (1)
Committee of Correspondence (1)
Committee of Public Safety (1, 2)
Continental Congress (First and Second)
Continental Dollar

Dartmouth (1)
Declaration of Independence
flintlock musket (1,2)
French and Indian War
The Intolerable Acts (1)
Olive Branch Petition
The Port Act (1)

Proclamation of 1763
The Quartering Act
Stamp Act (1)
The Sugar Act
The Tea Act
The Townshend Acts
Treaty of Paris

(1) mentioned in *Johnny Tremain*   (2) mentioned in *The Fighting Ground*

Revolutionary War Thought Bank

To stimulate class discussion and diary, provide your students with speeches, songs, and quotations from the Revolutionary War period to which they can respond.

Here are a few ideas:

* Read all of, or excerpts from *The Declaration of Independence* and *Common Sense.*

* Read, listen to, or perform the lyrics of songs that were popular during the Revolutionary War. (See Bibliography on page 78.)

* Encourage students to select quotations from the time of the Revolutionary War from both nonfiction and historical fiction sources.

Examples

"The sun never shined on a cause of greater worth. 'Tis not the affair of a city, a country, a province, or a kingdom, but of a continent—at least one eighth part of the habitable globe. 'Tis not the concern of a day, a year, or an age; posterity are virtually involved in the contest, and will be more or less affected, even to the end of time, by the proceedings now."

–Thomas Paine

"Don't fire unless fired upon! But if they want a war, let it begin here."

–Jonas Parker

"I know not what course others may take, but as for me, give me liberty or give me death."

–Patrick Henry

"I only regret that I have but one life to lose for my country."

–Nathan Hale

". . For men and women and children all over the world. You were right, you tall, dark boy, for even as we shoot down the British soldiers we are fighting for rights such as they will be enjoying a hundred years from now . . . There shall be no more tyranny. A handful of men cannot seize power over thousands. A man shall choose who it is shall rule over him."

–James Otis

Johnny Tremain

"And hadn't Jonathan talked with his friends of war, battles old and new, strategies fit for major generals? And, having fought their wars, they had always won their glory, hadn't they?"

The Fighting Ground

40

Making a Big Book

When students make a Big Book, they recreate the story they have read in new and different ways, demonstrating their understanding of that story on many levels.

Directions

1. Explain to your students what a Big Book is.

2. Decide whether students will construct a Big Book individually, in a group, or as a class.

3. Have students select one of the following ways to construct their Big Book:

   * **Chapter-by-Chapter**

      Students take one chapter at a time from the original story and respond to their understanding of that chapter with a page or more in their Big Book. This could easily be a class project with individuals or small groups each assigned a chapter to do for the collective work.

   * **Larger Sections**

      Students take larger sections of major story developments and respond to their understanding of each section with a page or more in their Big Book. This could also be done as a class project, with a group of students assigned to each section of the book.

   * **Free Style**

      Students retell the story any way they want.

   * **Creative License**

      Students use the story they have read as a model to create a totally new story. This could be a sequel, or a story with new characters or a new setting.

4. Provide students with an ample supply of paper, cardboard, scissors, glue, and other book-making materials. You may even want to send a ''we need'' list home for materials.

5. Encourage students to be creative. Suggest that they make pages with interesting textures and/or cut-out or fold-out designs. The only limitations in making a Big Book are students' imaginations!

Model It

Sometimes you can get a better idea of what something is like when you make a **scale model** of it. When you make a scale model of something, you make it bigger or smaller than the real object. We usually make small things bigger and big things smaller.

Look at the picture in Box A. Recopy it smaller in Box B. Use the grid lines to help you.

Box A

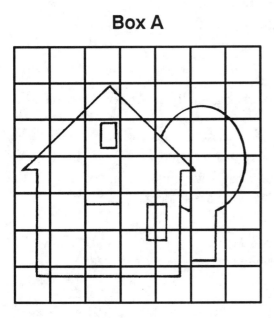

Box B

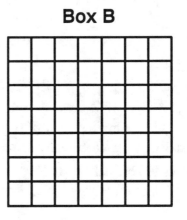

Working in a small group, look through books of the Revolutionary War period and find pictures of scenes in which you are interested such as the Boston Tea Party, Paul Revere's ride, or the winter at Valley Forge. Use papier-mâché, modeling clay, ice cream sticks and twigs, dried or silk plants, toy figures, paints, and other selected materials to create a scale model of one scene you have chosen.

Display your scenes for a parents' night or other meeting where others than those in your class can enjoy your work!

The Americans vs. the British

This is a fun way for students to learn or review facts about the Revolutionary War.

Directions

1. Divide the class evenly into Americans and British, with half the class sitting on either side.

2. Each team gets a set of numbered cards (0-9), as well as extra cards that it can distribute to its members.

   A student in each group should be assigned **one** of the numbered cards from the set (0-9). Then, depending on the size of the group, extra 0's, 1's, 2's and 3's may be assigned or left in a "grab pile" for students not assigned any of the original set of cards, or students not using their assigned cards to solve the problem.

   These are the cards (and quantity of cards) you will need to make for each team. You may want to make one set of cards white for the American team and the other set of cards red for the British team.

0 (5)	1 (2)	2 (1)	3 (2)	4 (1)
5 (2)	6 (1)	7 (2)	8 (1)	9 (1)

3. Give both sides time to work out their battle strategy—who will hold the cards, who will do the computations, and so forth. Explain that the side with the better strategy and use of cooperative teamwork will more likely win!

4. At the same time, give both sides a "fact-finder" (see page 44), which includes an incomplete fact about the Revolutionary War, as well as the mathematical problem that will help them complete the fact. You may give the fact finders orally or in written form.

5. As soon as a team solves the problem, members holding assigned numbers or extra cards must arrange themselves along their side of the room so that their answer is visible to the class.

6. If the teacher doesn't respond to the answer, it will mean that the answer is not correct, and those students must go back and rework the problem.

7. As soon as the teacher says, "That's correct!" the team that **first** correctly solved the problem gets one point.

8. The first team to get ten points wins!

The Americans vs. the British (cont.)

Here are some "fact finders" you can use for the Americans versus the British game.

1. Percentage of people who made their living by farming in the American colonies (30 x 18) ÷ 6	2. Year the British Parliament passed the Stamp Act (106 + 247) x 5	3. Number of colonists killed in the Boston Massacre 250250 ÷ 25 ÷ 1001 ÷ 2	4. Number of chests of tea that were dumped overboard during the Boston Tea Party 2040 ÷ 6
5. The number of people in 1775 who lived in Philadelphia, the largest city in Colonial America 200 x 200	6. Percentage of colonists who were Patriots (424 - 386) + (163 + 97) - (81 + 184)	7. Date of the beginning of the American Revolution (84632 + 83039) x 25	8. Number of American men and women who died when the first shots were fired at Lexington 4096 ÷ 64 ÷ 8
9. Date George Washington was made the Continental Army's commander-in-chief 24,607,100 ÷ 4	10. Population in the Thirteen Colonies by 1776 10 x 2 x 25 x 5 x 50 x 10 x 2	11. Number of German prisoners that were taken by Washington in the Battle of Trenton 12+452+9+321+ 75+31	12. Number of British soldiers who laid down their arms at Yorktown 4 x 20 x 100
13. Difference between the highest number of British and American soldiers fighting at one time (British) 50,000 - 18,000 (American)	14. Approximate number of Patriots killed in the Revolutionary War battles (9x8) x (76+24)	15. Approximate number of Patriots wounded in the Revolutionary War battles (2891+7540) - (957+1274)	16. Approximate number of Patriots who died of disease, exposure, or malnutrition during the Revolutionary War 10 x 10 x 10 x 10
17. Approximate number of Patriots who died in British prison camps during the Revolutionary War 420 + 675 + 3570 + 2914 + 99 + 822	18. Date that marked the official end of the Revolutionary War 16,772, 094 ÷ 18	19. Number of years the American Revolution lasted (15+23+42+16) ÷ (27-15)	20. Amount of money that Thomas Jefferson estimated the war cost (in millions of dollars) 23520 ÷ 7 ÷ 8 ÷ 3

44

Where Did It Happen?

For this activity you will need a United States and a European map with clearly marked latitude and longitude lines.

Draw a line to match each place with its grid point. Then write the matching pairs as answers to the questions at the bottom of the page.

London	47° N 71° W
West Point	36° N 80° W
Yorktown	41° N 74° W
Paris	37oN 76oW
Boston	35° N 82° W
Savannah	49° N 2° E
Cowpens	43° N 74° W
Guilford Courthouse	42° N 71° W
Quebec	32° N 81° W
Saratoga	51° N 0° PRIME MERIDIAN

1. Treaty that officially ended the war was signed here.
   Place_____Grid Point _____
2. Cornwallis surrendered to Washington here.
   Place_____Grid Point _____
3. In this place, Richard Montgomery and Benedict Arnold lost to the British.
   Place_____Grid Point _____
4. This major Southern port was held by the British.
   Place_____Grid Point _____
5. Victory here convinced France that the Americans could win in a war against the British.
   Place_____Grid Point _____
6. Soon after this battle, Cornwallis decided to leave North Carolina.
   Place_____Grid Point _____
7. This is where the taxes for the North American colonists were decided.
   Place_____Grid Point _____
8. Patriots dressed as Indians and dumped tea into this city's harbor.
   Place_____Grid Point _____
9. Benedict Arnold asked George Washington to give him command of this defensive post.
   Place_____Grid Point _____
10. The riflemen of the Southern Army won a battle in this cattle-grazing area.
    Place_____Grid Point _____

The Shortest Route

What if Paul Revere were to make his famous ride from Boston to Lexington on the roads that are available in Massachusetts today?

Look at the map below and determine the shortest route from Boston to Lexington using the roads marked on the map. Compute the distance in miles. Then, estimate how long it would take Paul Revere to:

(**Hint:** distance + rate = time)

1. drive this distance in a (car traveling at 55 mph) _____

2. ride it on a horse (traveling at 15 mph) _____

3. walk it at a brisk pace (traveling at 4 mph) _____

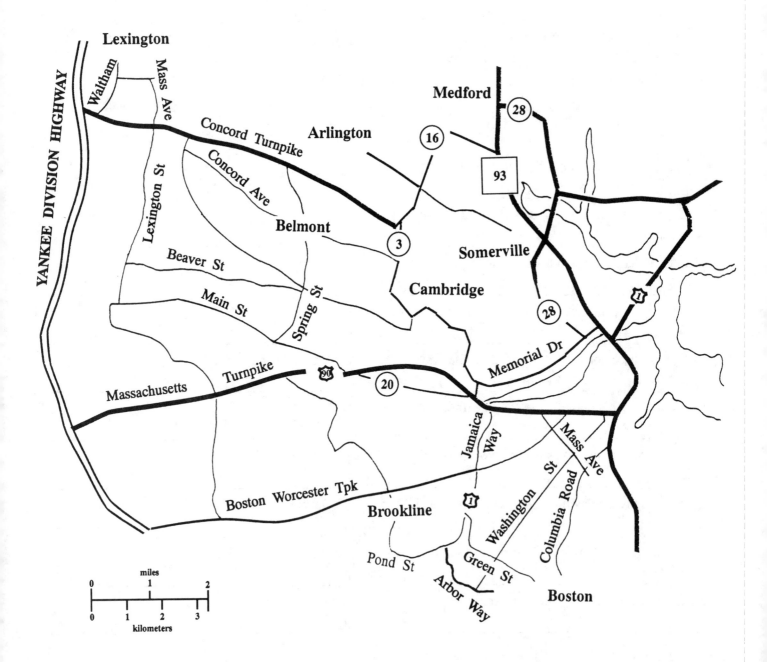

Natural Housing

The house Jonathan and the Hessians stayed in was a Swedish-style house,

> **" . . .made of logs, chinked with decaying clay, and clogged**
> **with clods of moss. In front of the doorway a shallow covered**
> **porch ran the full width of the house . . .**
>
> **It was a one-room house with a dirt floor, one oil-papered window, and**
> **a hearth at the far side."**

The "Swedish-style" log cabin mentioned in *The Fighting Ground* was the type of log cabin that we associate with the log cabins of Colonial America.

As a small group project, construct a model of a log cabin using only the materials you can find easily on the ground, such as twigs, broken branches, pine needles, mud, clay, and clods of decomposing plant material. Do not kill any plants to make your house!

Display your natural housing creations in a colonial home show!

Ben Franklin–Scientist

Benjamin Franklin was a great American. He had many outstanding accomplishments in his lifetime. He was a printer, a publisher, a writer, an inventor, a scientist, a diplomat, a statesman, and an inspiration to those he met.

At age 42, Franklin decided to devote himself to the study of science. During this time, he was recognized as one of the world's greatest scientists, inventing and experimenting, and loving his work. He proved that lightning was electricity and that things could be positively or negatively charged with electricity. Among the many things he made were the world's first battery, lighting rod, bifocal glasses, as well as an energy-efficient wood-burning stove. However, he never patented any of his inventions. He preferred, instead, to share what he had learned freely with the world.

Do some or all of these Franklin-related projects.

* Investigate the nature of electricity. Study the concepts of positive and negative as they relate to electricity. Do **not** fly a kite in a storm!

* Make a battery.

* Examine a pair of bifocal glasses. Research how and why they work to help in both nearsightedness and farsightedness.

* Franklin experimented with lime and plaster of Paris to increase the productivity of soil. Analyze how and why fertilizer works to make soil more productive.

* Franklin discovered that dark colors absorb heat, and light colors reflect heat. Investigate this principle.

* Research why his wood-burning stove (the Franklin stove) used energy more efficiently that the fireplaces that were being used during this time.

* Investigate some of the other scientific investigations he made, such as the rise of tides, the movement of the Gulf Stream in the Atlantic Ocean, and the increase of disease in poorly ventilated rooms.

* After ten years as a scientist, inventor, and writer of educational materials, Benjamin Franklin was pulled away from the work he loved. His country needed him. He played a major role in the Revolutionary War. Find out more about his life as a Patriot.

Endurance

Jonathan had to carry a twelve-pound musket for long time. For him, that was a considerable amount of weight to carry. It took a great deal of endurance.

How long can you hold something that weighs twelve pounds before it starts to feel heavy?

Directions

1. Get a large plastic bag and fill it with twelve pounds of potatoes.
2. Hold the bag over your shoulder as you walk around the playground. Have someone time you.
3. When you can't hold the bag any longer, put it down.
4. Mark down the length of time you held the bag.
5. Compare your time to ten other students in the class.
6. Make a bar graph to compare your time with the others.

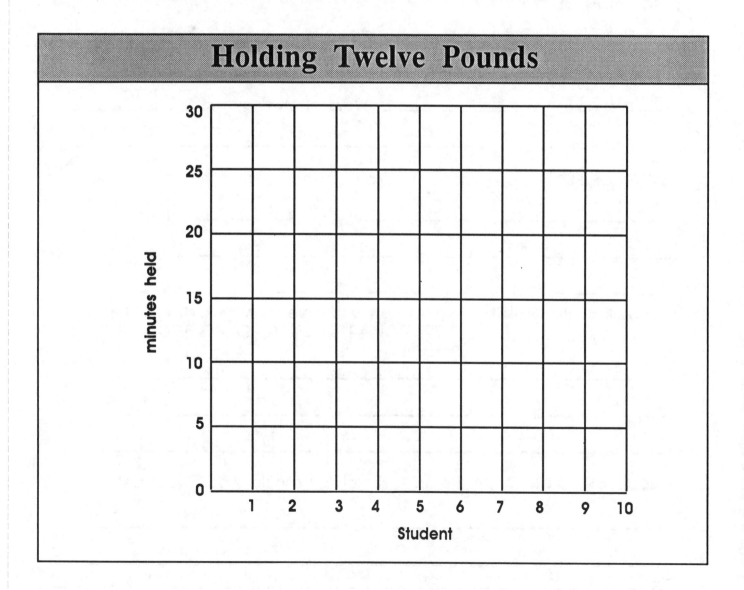

Pet Care

In *Johnny Tremain*, Goblin received excellent care from Johnny. Johnny loved this horse, and the care he gave Goblin demonstrated his love.

All pets need special care. Whether your pet is a horse like Johnny's, or a dog, cat, bird, fish, rodent, snake, or other animal, **you** are the one who is responsible for the care of the pet you have. Your pet **depends** on you!

Complete this pet care form for each of the pets you have.

My Pet

Name of Pet: _____

Type of Pet: _____

DESCRIPTION OF PET:

    Size: _____ **Age:** _____ **Sex:** _____

    Fur, Feather, Scale, or Skin Coloring: _____

    Eye Color: _____ **Ways of Moving:** _____

    Personality: _____

HISTORY OF PET: Write a brief description of where, when, how, and why you got this pet.

_____

_____

_____

PET CARE RESPONSIBILITIES: Explain how you care for your pet. Include such things as feeding, grooming, cleaning, and exercising.

_____

_____

_____

SPECIAL CHARACTERISTICS: Describe something special about your pet.

_____

_____

50

Revolutionary War Fact Finders

Revolutionary War Encyclopedia

Have students work in groups to create a Revolutionary War Encyclopedia. In their encyclopedias, students explain and illustrate people, places, events, and other things relating to the Revolutionary War Word Bank found on page 39.

Scavenger Hunt

Divide the class into groups of two or three. Distribute a different scavenger hunt list to each group (page 54). Each group will use classroom and library resources to complete their hunt. When all have finished, answers may be shared with the class.

Revolutionary War Game Board

In groups, students create their own Revolutionary War game boards.

Have students do the following:

* Name the game.

* Write directions for playing the game.

* Design the game board. (A blank game board is provided on pages 52 and 53.)

* Play the game.

* Teach another group to play the game.

To help them get started, bring in existing game boards to act as models. You may also give them suggestions for space labeling.

EXAMPLE

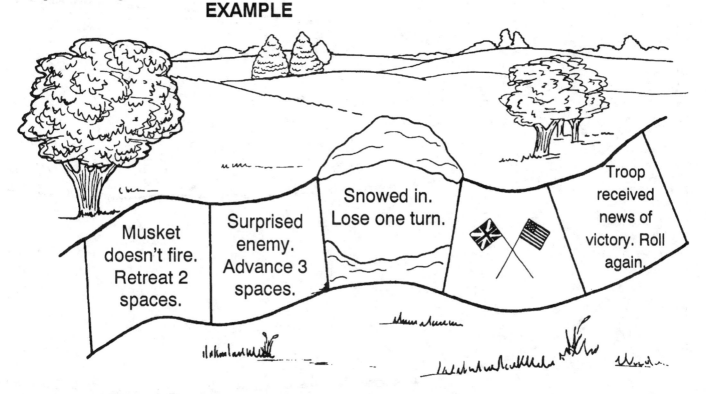

Revolutionary War Game Board

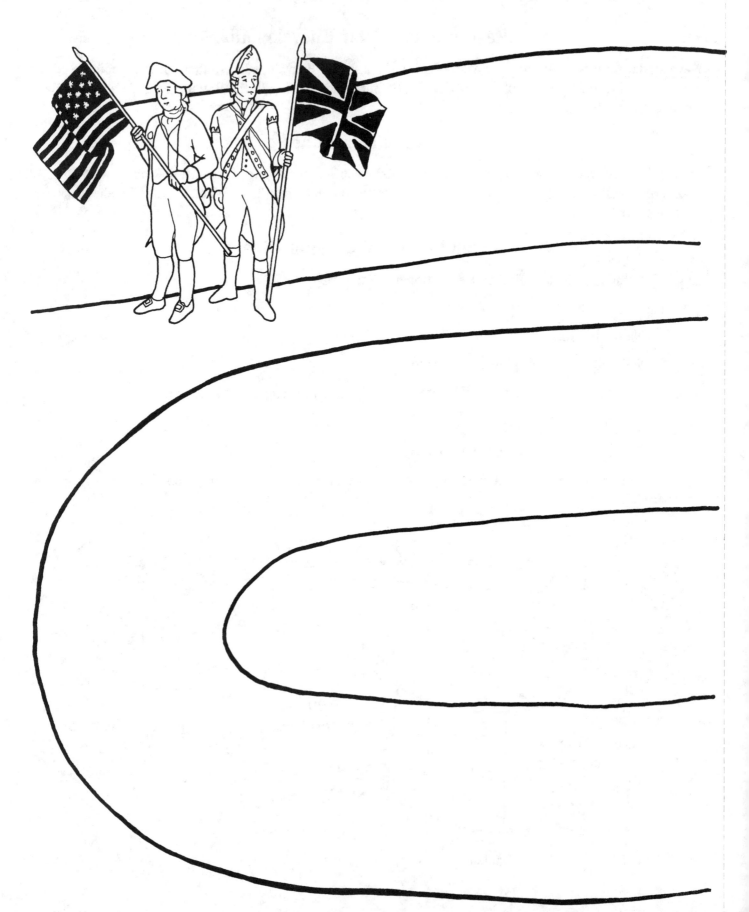

52

Revolutionary War Game Board *(cont.)*

Social Studies

Scavenger Hunt

Group 1

1. Describe the Proclamation of 1763 and its part in the causation of the Revolutionary War.
2. Prepare a short biography on King George III.
3. Explain what happened on December 16, 1773.
4. Define *boycott*.
5. What would have happened if King George III had allowed the American colonies representation in Parliament?

Group 2

1. Describe the Quartering and Stamp Acts and their parts in the causation of the Revolutionary War.
2. Prepare a short biography on Samuel Adams.
3. Explain what happened on April 19, 1775.
4. Define *Committees of Correspondence*.
5. What would have happened if the Olive Branch Petition proposed by the Second Continental Congress for a peaceful settlement with Great Britain had been honored?

Group 3

1. Describe the Townshend Acts and their part in the causation of the Revolutionary War.
2. Prepare a short biography on George Washington.
3. Explain what happened on June 17, 1775.
4. Define *minuteman*.
5. What would have happened if the American colonists had professional soldiers for their fighting?

Group 4

1. Describe the Boston Massacre and its part in the causation of the Revolutionary War.
2. Prepare a short biography on Thomas Paine.
3. Explain what happened on July 4, 1776.
4. Define *redcoat*.
5. What would have happened if modern-day guns were available to the soldiers who fought for both sides in the Revolutionary War?

Group 5

1. Describe the Boston Tea Party and its part in the causation of the Revolutionary War.
2. Prepare a short biography on Thomas Jefferson.
3. Explain what happened on October 6-19, 1781.
4. Define *Common Sense*.
5. What would have happened if Benjamin Franklin was unable to secure the help of the French in fighting the Revolutionary War?

Group 6

1. Describe the Intolerable Acts and their part in the causation of the Revolutionary War.
2. Prepare a short biography on Benjamin Franklin.
3. Explain what happened on September 3, 1783.
4. Define *flintlock musket*.
5. What would have happened if the colonists had lost the war?

Family Tree

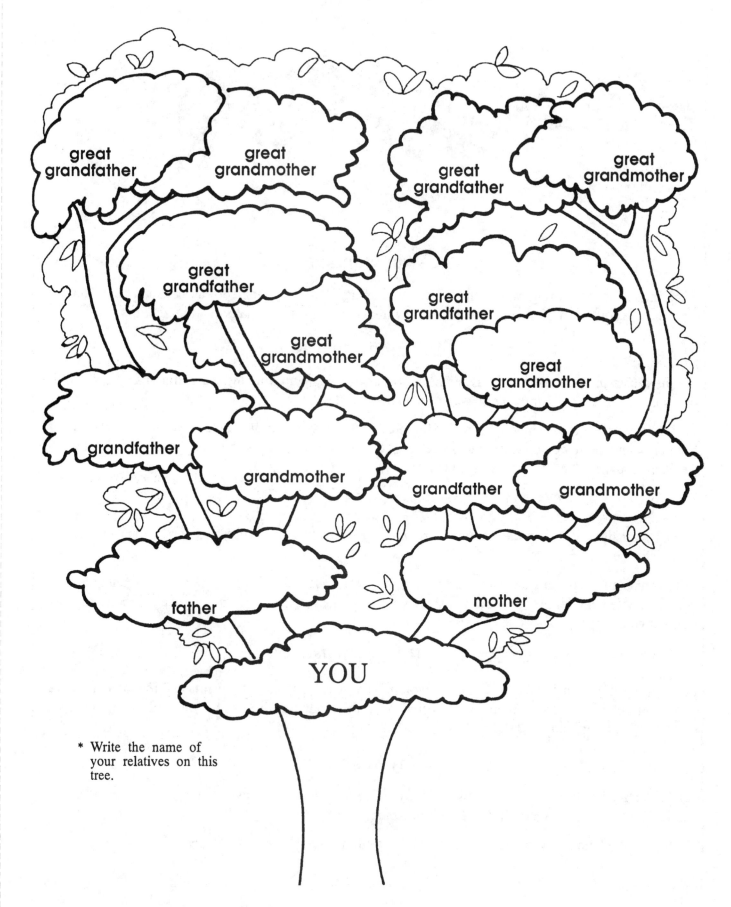

great grandfather

great grandmother

great grandfather

great grandmother

great grandfather

great grandmother

great grandfather

great grandmother

grandfather

grandmother

grandfather

grandmother

father

mother

YOU

* Write the name of your relatives on this tree.

Art Activities

War Montage

Work in groups, or with the whole class to create montages of wars using current, consumable resources. A montage is a collection of pictures, photos, and symbols put together to make one big picture.

Designing a Crest

In *Johnny Tremain*, the crest of the Lyte family was an eye rising up from the sea. From this eye, rays of light streamed out. The Lyte family motto was ''Let there be Lyte.''

Design a crest and create a motto that would be appropriate for your family. Make what you create meaningful. Your crest and motto could incorporate something of your family's history, philosophy, style or attitudes. Use the form on page 57 to help you design your crest and display your motto.

Family Heirloom

Johnny Tremain's silver cup was a family heirloom, a treasured possession passed down to him from his mother before she died.

Does your family have any treasured things that have been passed down from generation to generation? If so, draw or create a model of it to show and share with your class. Explain the importance this heirloom has for you and your family.

Picture This!

Many artists living during the time of the Revolutionary War chronicled the events and feelings of the war in pictures. Look at and discuss reproductions of some of these pictures that can be found in Revolutionary War books. (See bibliography, page 78.)

Clay Sculpture

Johnny Tremain fashioned wax models of things before he cast them in silver. He tried very hard to make the handles for the sugar basin to fill Mr. Hancock's order.

Work with modeling clay to make a sugar basin that might have pleased Mr. Hancock!

Designing a Crest

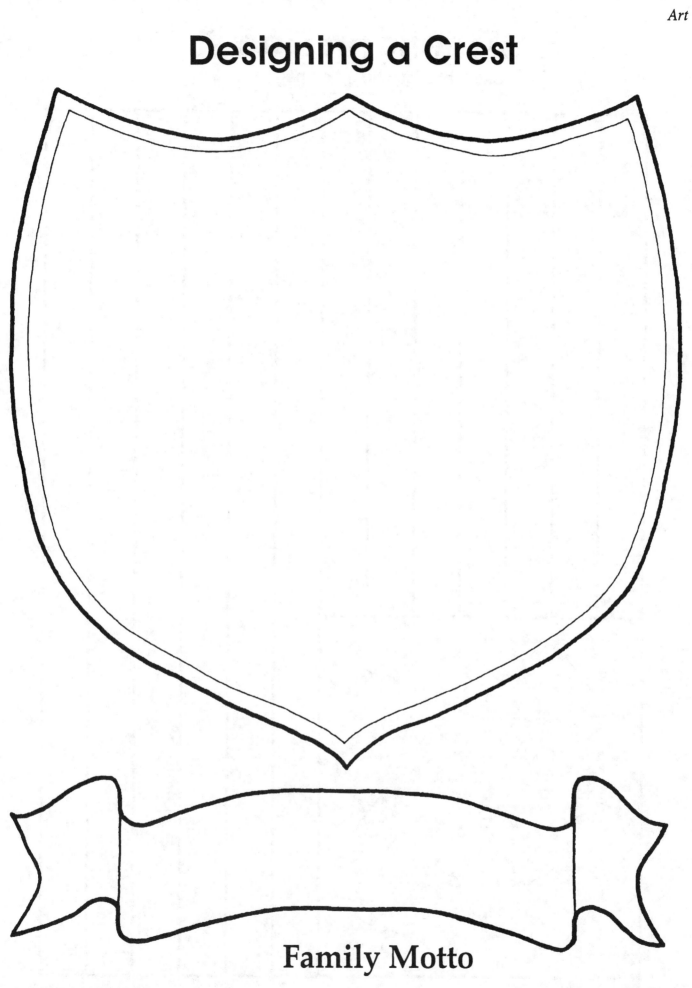

Family Motto

American Flag
Use for bulletin board on page 74.

58

British Flag
Use for bulletin board on page 74.

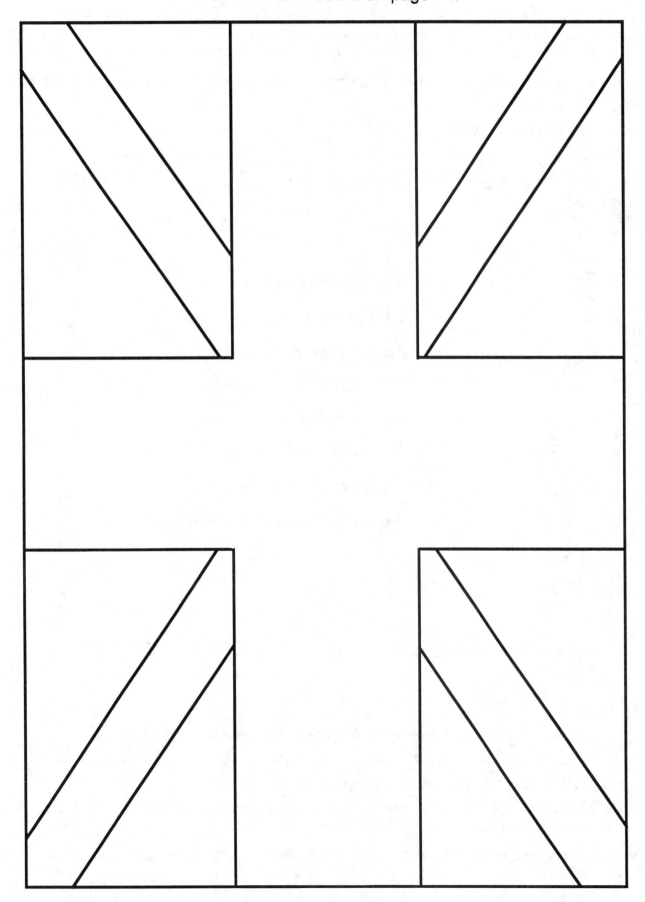

Yankee Doodle

Although it began as a British song used to make fun of the Americans, Yankee Doodle was adopted by the Americans as their own. They sang, whistled, and played it throughout the Revolutionary War. It could be heard as the British retreated from Concord as well as after their surrender at Yorktown.

It did not really matter which words were sung. Americans used the tune freely, composing their own lyrics for whatever the occasion called.

The version most people know is:

Yankee Doodle went to town,
Riding on a pony,
He stuck a feather in his cap
And called it macaroni.
Yankee Doodle keep it up,
Yankee Doodle dandy,
Mind the music and the step,
And with the girls be handy.

Directions

As a class or in groups, choose one or more of the following ways to perform Yankee Doodle.

1. **PLAY IT!** Use kazoos, combs with wax paper wrapped around them, or other musical instruments.

2. **WHISTLE IT!** See if your class can whistle together in unison.

3. **SING IT!** Compose your own lyrics to create a funny song about something that happened at your school, or in your classroom.

For any of these performance options, select a few students to add drums to create a more authentic sound.

Life on the Outside

"Johnny's life with the Laphams had been so limited he knew little of the political strife which was turning Boston into two armed camps."

–Johnny Tremain
"The Rising Eye"

In *Johnny Tremain,* an entire new world was opened to Johnny when he began his association with Rab and the Patriots. Life outside the Lapham's shop was much more complicated than he had imagined. Because of the exposure to ideas he received in his riding for *The Boston Observer* and the Boston Committee of Correspondence, Johnny became completely engaged in the issues that brought about the Revolutionary War.

Most of us experience the feeling that there is more to life than what we encounter in the smaller world of our everyday lives, the world in which we develop our values, our prejudices, and our aspirations. In such a world, we can become limited in what we know and experience by the boundaries of that world.

There are many ways to see and experience "life on the outside." Books can make us aware of cultures, ways of life, beliefs, attitudes, and ideas that are different from our own. By traveling to other places, observing what happens in and around these places, and speaking with the people we meet there, we can broaden our perspective. Taking the time to learn about the ways and ideas that are different from our own can only enrich our lives and help us live fuller, more compassionate lives. It is in our best interest and in the best interest of the world in which we live to learn more about "life on the outside."

* As a class, brainstorm ways through which we can learn more about "life on the outside."

* Read about many people, places, and things that are outside your experience.

* On a daily or weekly basis, work in groups to find out more about another way of life. Share what you have learned with the rest of the class.

* Invite people of different cultures to share their lifestyles with you.

* Keep a journal of your "Life on the Outside." In it, write the ideas that cross your mind as you are learning about new people, places, and things.

* Each day, write down one thing that you learned.

Johnnycake Recipe

There was a type of bread that was popular during and after the time of the Revolutionary War. It traveled well, staying edible for the length of a journey. This "journeycake" became known as **johnnycake**, and was often carried in the packs of soldiers because it traveled so well. Jonathan ate it in *The Fighting Ground*.

Here is what you will need to make some of your own johnnycake!

INGREDIENTS:

1 cup yellow cornmeal

1/4 cup sugar

1/2 teaspoon baking soda

1 teaspoon cream of tartar

1/4 teaspoon of salt

1 cup buttermilk

1 well-beaten egg

1 tablespoon molasses

1 tablespoon melted, unsalted butter

butter for greasing baking pan

Directions:

* Preheat oven to 425 degrees.

* Lightly grease an 8-inch square baking dish or pan.

* In a large mixing bowl, sift all the dry ingredients together.

* Add the buttermilk, beaten egg, molasses, and melted butter to the dry mixture. Mix until it is smooth.

* Pour this mixture into the baking container. Bake it for 30 minutes.

* After the johnnycake comes out of the oven, turn it upside down and remove it from the container. Let it cool slightly before you cut it into servings.

This johnnycake will serve 6 to 8 people.

Interact

In *Johnny Tremain,* Johnny is faced with choices that involve his ways of interacting with people. He makes choices that anger or offend some people, and choices that please or inspire others. He learns that the way he responds to people has a direct impact on his relationships with these people.

The way we choose to interact with others can nurture or destroy our chances for relationships. The choices we make can greatly affect our future. It is important to make those choices that reflect the people we really are or would like to be.

Directions

Divide into small groups. Each group will select one of the interaction cards on this page to dramatize for the class. Each situation needs to have a positive ending for all the characters who are a part of the dramatization.

A student who is very good at sports is approached by another student with little skill at sports. He/she wants to be on the skilled player's team.	An older sister is very worried that her younger sister is being wrongly influenced by a person who is not a member of the family. The younger sister loves this person.
Several boys who are always fighting have made the class a very difficult place to be. The teacher decides that something must be done to ease the tension in the classroom.	One person who has a reputation for having a fierce temper is tripped accidentally by another person. A bystander witnesses the fall.
One girl (or boy) has more friends than another person. This person is very jealous of the more popular person. The jealous person has a chance to spread rumors about the more popular person.	A child at a party has horrible manners. The behavior he exhibits is making others around him move away. The host of the party decides to intervene.

Famous People of the Revolutionary War

Directions

1. Divide the class into small groups and give each group a different portrait of the famous people on this page and on page 65. Add additional famous people if you desire.

2. Have each group write a short biography of its famous person. Use the Famous Person form (page 66) for the final draft.

3. When each group has completed its page, assemble the pages into a book. Students may use any of the portraits to create a cover or design one of their own. Entitle your class book "Famous People of the Revolutionary War" and display it in your classroom. Have each group present an oral report to the class about its famous person.

| Emma Sampson | Martha Washington | Abigail Smith Adams |
| Molly Pitcher | Crispus Attucks | Sybil Ludington |

Famous People Portraits

Directions

Cut out these portraits of famous people and give one to each group. They will be used for your classroom's "Famous People of The Revolutionary War" book. (See page 64.)

Patrick Henry

Thomas Paine

Paul Revere

Samuel Adams

George Washington

John Hancock

John Adams

Benjamin Franklin

Thomas Jefferson

Nathanael Greene

Famous Person

Colony Sign-Up!

See page 72 for directions.

The New England Colonies

☐ New Hampshire _____

☐ Massachusetts _____

☐ Rhode Island _____

☐ Connecticut _____

The Middle Colonies

☐ New York _____

☐ Pennsylvania _____

☐ New Jersey _____

☐ Delaware _____

The Southern Colonies

☐ Maryland _____

☐ Virginia _____

☐ North Carolina _____

☐ South Carolina _____

☐ Georgia _____

Important Event Cards

Cut out these cards and distribute them according to the directions on page 69.

October, 1763	**May, 1765**	**1767**	**March 5, 1770**
December 16, 1773	**June 1, 1774**	**September 5 to October 26, 1774**	**April 19, 1775**
June 15, 1775	**June 17, 1775**	**January, 1776**	**July 4, 1776**
December 26, 1776	**September 11, 1777**	**October 17, 1777**	**February 6, 1778**
August 16, 1780	**January 17, 1781**	**October 19, 1781**	**September 3, 1783**

Important Event!

Directions

1. Assign one or more Important Event Cards (page 68) to each group until all events have been assigned. Additional dates may be added at your discretion.

2. Instruct students to research the date and determine what special event of the Revolutionary War took place on that date.

3. Have students complete a written summary of the event that will be **neatly** copied onto the Important Event! form below. Students should include as much of the Who, What, Why, Where, When, and How of the event as they can.

4. Arrange the graphics into a timeline for the unit management bulletin board, Independence. Directions are on pages 74 and 75.

Important Event!

Date: _____

Summary:

Unit Management Overview

Purpose

The activities presented in this unit management section are designed to focus student learning of the people, places, and events of the Revolutionary War period, as well as provide a showcase for student work. Students may work individually, as partners, or in small groups to complete the activities.

Components

Research Center (pages 72 and 73)

A center which students may use to work individually or in small groups to complete Revolutionary War unit activities.

Bulletin Board (pages 74 and 75)

A visual display that identifies the causes of the Revolutionary War, locations of the thirteen colonies and surrounding lands, as well as important events, famous people, and important facts about the colonies.

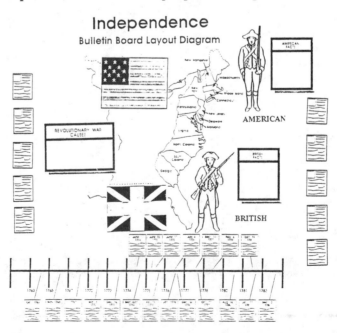

Independence
See page 72 for directions.

Independence *(cont.)*

A Research Center of People, Places, and Events of The Revolutionary War

Preparation

1. Construct your center according to the Research Center Layout Diagram (page 73). Remember, your research center may be used year after year, so any extra time you put into it now—coloring and laminating graphics, and so forth—will pay off later!

2. Collect as many reference materials on the Revolutionary War period as you can. See the Bibliography (page 78) for a partial listing of age-appropriate titles. Your school and local libraries are another excellent source.

3. Reproduce the Famous People of the Revolutionary War montage (page 64) on heavy paper. Color it and cut it out around the outside lines of the artwork. Attach it to the middle section of the center. Also reproduce and attach (according to the layout diagram on page 73) Colony Sign-Up! (page 67), Independence (page 71), as well as American Flag (page 58) and British Flag (page 59).

4. Copy any other center graphics as shown in the layout diagram.

Procedure

Introduce the center to the class and explain each area of the centers.

Colony Sign-Up

Using the map graphic for Independence (page 71), students working in groups will select a colony they would like to research and report on.

Once a colony has been selected, put a star sticker in the square in front of the colony's name on the Colony Sign-up sheet (page 67), to show that a colony has been taken. Then, write the names of the people in the group selecting that colony on the lines after the colony's name.

Groups are to present reports to the class that explain their colony's participation in the Revolutionary War, as well as other noteworthy events that took place in the colony during that time.

Revolutionary War Library

Students and groups may use these reference materials for any of their projects or activities.

American and British Flags

Using the pattern you have made available at the center, each student or group is to make both flags of the Revolutionary War (pages 58 and 59) using markers, pieces of material, sticks, and paper scraps. Encourage students to use different construction styles, such as mosaic, geometrical shapes, patchwork pieces, and paper balls, in addition to markers and crayons to complete their flags. The completed flags can then be displayed in the classroom. Some may be used to decorate the unit management bulletin board.

Other Activities

You may also want to use the center as a resource for completing many of the other activities found throughout the book. Some of these you may want to include on a rotating basis at (not necessarily attached to) the center. Possible additions to the center might be the forms for Important Event! (page 69) and Famous Person (page 66), as well as the materials and directions for completing the Revolutionary War Game Board (pages 51 to 53).

Independence *(cont.)*

Research Center Layout Diagram

INDEPENDENCE
Research Center

At this center you will:

1. Research a colony.
2. Profile a famous person.
3. Report on an important event.
4. Make a British and an American flag.
5. Complete other Revolutionary War-related activities.

To make this center you will need:

3 sheets of poster board (you may wish to back with cardboard)

3 9" x 12" manila mailing envelopes

1 5" x 7" manila mailing envelope

1 small manila envelope to hold stickers

13 stickers

Revolutionary War reference materials (See Bibliography for a partial list)

lots of paper scraps

lots of material scraps

markers

1 Independence Map (cut out)

1 Colony Sign-Up! chart

10 Famous Person forms

20 Important Event forms

1 Famous People Montage (cut out)

British Flag pattern (one per student)

American Flag pattern (one per student)

2 dowels to display flags

Independence *(cont.)*

A Bulletin Board of People, Places, and Events of The Revolutionary War

Preparation

1. Select an area in the room where students can assemble the bulletin board as the unit progresses.
2. Construct the bulletin board according to the Bulletin Board Layout Diagram on page 75.

Helpful Hints:

*   Staple background paper to bulletin board.

*   Make transparencies on pages 58, 59, 71, 76, and 77.

*   Enlarge those graphics to desired size using an overhead projector. (See Bulletin Board Layout Diagram for suggested proportions.) Then trace and color them accordingly.

    If you would like any of the graphics to appear three-dimensional, first cut out additional outlines of the soldiers and flags from black construction paper. Arrange them on the bulletin board where you would like them to be, using pushpins with ''flat'' plastic ends. Next, put a small drop of glue on the tips of the pushpins (do one graphic at a time), wait about a minute for the glue to set up, then attach your colored graphics to the pushpins, directly over their black outlines. Your soldiers and flags will look like they have shadows!

*   Prepare ''Information Posters'' for Revolutionary War Causes, British Facts, and American Facts (See layout diagram.) Fill in these posters as your study of the Revolutionary War progresses.

Here are some areas you may want to include on your posters:

Reasons for War	**Views on British Rule**	**Major Victories**
Ways of Life	**Important Leaders**	**Resources**
Economy	**Uniforms**	**Casualties**
Government	**Hardships**	**Views of War**
Foreign Aid	**Weapons**	**Treaty of Paris**

74

Independence *(cont.)*

Bulletin Board Layout Diagram

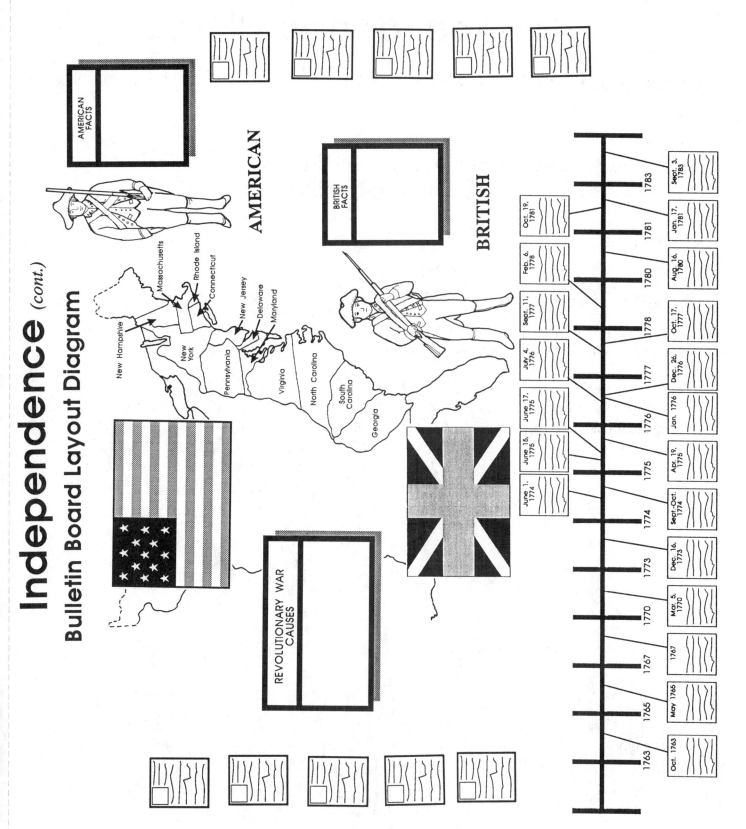

AMERICAN FACTS

AMERICAN

BRITISH FACTS

BRITISH

REVOLUTIONARY WAR CAUSES

New Hampshire · Massachusetts · Rhode Island · Connecticut · New York · New Jersey · Delaware · Maryland · Pennsylvania · Virginia · North Carolina · South Carolina · Georgia

1763 · 1765 · 1767 · 1770 · 1773 · 1774 · 1775 · 1776 · 1777 · 1778 · 1780 · 1781 · 1783

Oct. 1763 · May 1765 · 1767 · Mar. 5, 1770 · Dec. 16, 1773 · Sept.–Oct. 1774 · Apr. 19, 1775 · Jan. 1776 · Dec. 26, 1776 · Oct. 17, 1777 · Aug. 16, 1780 · Jan. 17, 1781 · Sept. 3, 1783

June 1, 1774 · June 15, 1775 · June 17, 1775 · July 4, 1776 · Sept. 11, 1777 · Feb. 6, 1778 · Oct. 19, 1781

An American Soldier

A British Soldier

Bibliography

Bliven, Bruce, Jr. *American Revolution, 1760-1783.* (Random House, 1981)

Bliven, Bruce, Jr. *The American Revolution.* (Random House, 1986)

Fritz, Jean. *And Then What Happened Paul Revere?* (Coward, 1973)

Fritz, Jean. *What's the Big Idea, Ben Franklin?* (Coward, 1976)

Fritz, Jean. *Why Don't You Get A Horse, Sam Adams?* (Coward, 1974)

Fritz, Jean. *Will You Sign Here, John Hancock?* (Coward, 1976)

Hirsch, S. Carl. *Famous American Revolutionary War Heroes.* (Rand McNally & Company, 1974)

Ingraham, Leonard W. *An Album of the American Revolution.* (Franklin Watts, 1971)

Jefferson, Thomas. *The Declaration of Independence,* as presented in the *American Tradition in Literature,* edited by Sculley Bradley, Richmond Croom Beaty, and E. Hudson Long (W.W. Norton & Company, Inc., 1967)

Knight, James E. *Boston Tea Party: Rebellion in the Colonies.* (Troll, 1982)

Lancaster, Bruce. *The American Revolution.* (Doubleday, 1957)

Lloyd, Ruth and Norman. *The American Heritage Songbook.* (American Heritage Publishing Co., Inc., 1969)

Longfellow, Henry Wadsworth. (Ted Rand, illus.) *Paul Revere's Ride.* (Dutton Children's Book, 1990)

McDowell, Bart. *The Revolutionary War: America's Fight For Freedom.* (National Geographic Society, 1967)

McGoven, Ann. *The Secret Soldier: The Story of Deborah Sampson.* (Scholastic, 1975)

Mollo, John. *Uniforms of the American Revolution.* (Macmillan, 1975)

Morris, Richard B. *The American Revolution.* (Lerner, 1985)

Paine, Thomas. *Common Sense and The American Crisis,* as presented in *The American Tradition in Literature,* edited by Sculley Bradley, Richmond Croom Beatty, and E. Hudson Long. (W.W. Norton & Company, Inc., 1967)

Rand, Ted. Illustrator. *Henry Wadsworth Longfellow Paul Revere's Ride.* (Dutton Children's Book, 1990)

Reeder, Russell P. *Bold Leaders of the American Revolution.* (Little, Brown, 1973)

Richards, Norman. *The Story of the Declaration of Independence.* (Children's Press, 1968)

Scott, John Anthony. *History of the American People.* (Facts On File, 1990)

Stein, R. Conrad. *The Story of Lexington and Concord.* (Children's Press, 1983)

Suter, Joanne. *U.S. History: Beginning of a Nation.* (Panthera Press, 1990)

Historical Fiction

Avi. *The Fighting Ground.* (Harper & Row, 1984)

Benchley, Nathaniel. *George the Drummer Boy.* (Harper & Row, 1977)

Benchley, Nathaniel. *Sam the Minuteman.* (Harper & Row, 1969)

Clapp, Patricia. *I'm Deborah Sampson: A Soldier in the War of the Revolution.* (Lothrop, 1977)

Collier, James Lincoln and Christopher Collier. *My Brother Sam Is Dead.* (Scholastic, 1974)

Forbes, Esther. *Johnny Tremain.* (Dell, 1970)

Forbes, Esther. *Paul Revere and the World He Lived In.* (Houghton, 1962)

Lawson, Robert. *Ben and Me.* (Little, Brown & Company, 1988)

O'Dell, Scott. *Sarah Bishop.* (Scholastic, 1980)

Answer Key

Page 9

1. Johnny learned to count to ten before he reacted. This ten second period gave him time to "cool off."
2. Because Johnny did not "blow-up" at the black girl who accidently threw water on him, he met and befriended Sam Adams, and was hired by this man to ride for the Boston Committee of Correspondence.

Page 12

Johnny's self-consciousness about his hand drew the attention of other people to it. His shame and disgust at his disfigurement led others to "reflect" his attitude. At the dance, he forgot entirely about his hand and had a wonderful time. The girls he danced with did not seem to notice his hand had been crippled. As Rab told him, it was Johnny himself who put the notion of "crippled-ness" into the heads of others.

Page 15

Accept reasonable answers.

Page 21

father: "Don't you - by God - don't you go beyond!"

mother: "Just find out! Then come on right back! You hear?"

Page 22

Tavern: two miles north of Rocktown

Alexandria: ten miles to the northwest of the tavern

Flemington: six miles northeast of the tavern

Linvale: four miles south of the tavern

Pennington: seven miles south of the tavern

Rocktown: two miles south of tavern, the highest point on the road

Snydertown: three miles east of Rocktown

Trenton: twenty miles south of the tavern

Well's Ferry: west of the tavern on the big river

Jonathan's route: He starts at the tavern and heads south through Rocktown and almost reaches Linvale. He returns to the tavern by the same route.

Page 23

1. Mercenaries are soldiers who fight for money.
2. The Hessians were from Germany.
3. The Hessians had a brutal reputation. They had bayoneted the wounded American soldiers at Long Island.
4. Answers should reflect Jonathan's vacillation about who and what the "enemy" is.
5. Not all the Hessians seemed to view Jonathan the same way. Answers might reflect this. Accept any responses that are appropriate and supported.
6. Jonathan realized that the "people" fighting the war were not the war. He showed compassion for them as they had done for him. Accept any appropriate responses.

Page 27

Accept reasonable answers.

Page 38

To make a wordsearch puzzle, write the list of chosen words across, down, backwards, and diagonally on the grid provided. Instruct puzzle makers to fill in the remaining spaces with their choice of letters. To do the puzzle, circle the words as you find them

Page 44

1. nearly 90%	2. 1765	3. 5	4. about 340
5. 40,000	6. less than 33%	7. 4/19/1775	8. 8
9. 6/15/1775	10. 2,500,000	11. over 900	12. 8,000
13. 32,000	14. 7,200	15. 8,200	16. 10,000
17. 8,500	18. 9/3/1783	19. 8	20. 140 million

Answer Key (cont.)

Page 45

Paris, 49°N 2°E; Yorktown, 37°N 76°W; Quebec, 47°N 71°W; Savannah, 32°N 81°W; Saratoga, 43°N 74°W; Guilford Courthouse, 36°N 80°W; London, 51°N 0° Prime Meridian; Boston, 42°N 71°W; West Point, 41°N 74°W; Cowpens, 35°N 82°W

Page 46

Accept reasonable answers.

Page 54

Group 1

1. The colonists resented the British government telling them where they could and could not settle.
2. Ask the group to present their biography for the class with as much creativity and dramatics as they can!
3. The Boston Tea Party should be described in detail.
4. *Boycott* means to refuse to buy, sell, or use.
5. Accept reasonable answers.

Group 2

1. With the Quartering Act, colonists were forced to house and feed British soldiers. With the Stamp Act, colonists were forced to pay for a tax stamp on a number of printed things.
2. Ask the group to ''present'' their biography. (See #2 above).
3. The Battles of Lexington and Concord should be described.
4. A *Committee of Correspondence* is a network of letter writers used to spread news of interest to the Patriots, explaining how British actions were a threat to American liberties.
5. Accept reasonable answers.

Group 3

1. With the Townshend Acts, taxes from the British government were replaced with ''duties'' on the things the colonists imported. These duties were just ''disguised'' taxes, and the colonists were angered.
2. Ask the group to ''present'' their biography.
3. The Battle of Bunker Hill should be described.
4. *Minutemen* were Patriots ready to fight on a ''minute's'' notice.
5. Accept reasonable answers.

Group 4

1. Although the Boston Massacre was caused by the violence of a crowd of Americans protesting British taxation without representation, the ''self-defense'' killing of the protesters was used to turn public opinion against the British.
2. Ask the group to ''present'' their biography.
3. The adoption of *The Declaration Of Independence* should be described.
4. A *redcoat* is a red-coated British soldier.
5. Accept reasonable answers.

Group 5

1. With the Boston Tea Party, Patriots let the British government know that any taxation without representation, however small, was unacceptable.
2. Ask the group to ''present'' their biography.
3. The Battle of Yorktown and Cornwallis surrender should be described.
4. *Common Sense* was a pamphlet written by Thomas Paine that stirred the colonists to believe in their right to liberty.
5. Accept reasonable answers.

Group 6

1. With the Intolerable Acts, Boston and the entire state of Massachusetts was ''punished'' by the King. They lost many of their political rights, as well as found their main supply center, the Fort of Boston, closed. Other states could fare the same fate if the Intolerable Acts were allowed to remain.
2. Ask the group to ''present'' their biography.
3. The signing of the Treaty of Paris should be explained.
4. A *flintlock musket* was a weapon used by many soldiers in fighting the Revolutionary War.
5. Accept reasonable answers.

Page 69

Oct., 1763–Proclamation of 1763; May, 1765–Colonists receive news of passage of Stamp Act; 1767–Passage of Townshend Acts; March 5, 1770–Boston Massacre; Dec. 16, 1773–Boston Tea Party;

June 1, 1774–Port of Boston is closed to commerce because of tea destroyed during Boston Tea Party;

Sept. 5—Oct. 26, 1774–First Continental Congress meets; April 19, 1775–Battles of Lexington and Concord (Minutemen and Redcoats); June 15, 1775–Second Continental Congress names George Washington as Commander-in-Chief of Continental Army; June 17, 1775–Bunker Hill captured by British; Jan., 1776–Thomas Paine's *Common Sense*; July 4, 1776– *Declaration of Independence* adopted; Dec. 26, 1776–Washington crosses Delaware River into Trenton, New Jersey, and makes surprise attack on Hessians; Sept. 11, 1777–Washington's army beaten by British at Brandywine, British troops occupy Philadelphia; Oct. 17, 1777–Burgoyne surrenders at Saratoga; Feb. 6, 1776–France signs alliance with U.S.; Aug. 16, 1780–British defeat Americans at Camden; Jan. 17, 1781–Americans win victory at Cowpens; Oct. 19, 1781–Cornwallis surrenders at Yorktown; Sept. 3, 1783–The United States and Great Britain sign what is called ''The Treaty of Paris,'' in Paris, France.